Dark Angels
of Light

Dark Angels of Light

Dr. David Allen Lewis

New Leaf Press

P.O. BOX 311, GREEN FOREST, AR 72638

FIRST EDITION, 1985

Cover art:
Paul Fornier

Typesetting by SPACE
(Sharp Printing & Computer Enterprise)
Berryville, AR

Library of Congress Catalog Number: 84-061915
ISBN: 0-89221-117-2

Table Of Contents

Chapter 1. Characteristics of a Cult 9

Chapter 2. Network of Light 15

Chapter 3. The New Christ 23

Chapter 4. Mormonism 33

Chapter 5. Jehovah's Witnesses 41

Chapter 6. Christian Science 49

Chapter 7. Man-Centered Cults 57

Chapter 8. Pseudo-Christian Cults 65

Chapter 9. The Unification Church 75

Chapter 10. Eastern Religions 85

Chapter 11. TM: Relaxation or Religion? 93

Chapter 12. TM Instructor Finds Christ 101

Chapter 13. Satanism and Witchcraft 105

Chapter 14. A Matter of Life and Death 115

Chapter 15. The Road to Endor 123

Chapter 16. Reaching the Cultist with the Gospel 129

Appendix: Sources of More Information 136

"Scripture Describing Cover Art"

. . . "that man of sin be revealed, the son of perdition;" II Thessalonians 2:3

". . . then shall that Wicked be revealed," II Thessalonians 2:8

"Even him, whose coming is after the working of Satan with all power and signs and lying wonders. And with all deceivableness of unrighteousness" . . . II Thessalonians 2:9-10

". . . the dragon (Satan) gave him his power, and his seat, and great authority." Revelation 13:2

". . . and all the world wondered after the beast." Revelation 13:3

". . . and power was given him over all kindreds, and tongues, and nations. And all that dwell upon the earth shall worship him, whose names are not written in the book of life of the Lamb slain from the foundation of the world." Revelation 13:7-8

". . .he doeth great wonders, so that he maketh fire come down from heaven on the earth in the sight of men, and deceiveth them that dwell on the earth by the means of those miracles which he had power to do in the sight of the beast . . ." Revelation 13:13-14

Chapter 1

Characteristics of a Cult

A few decades ago, in less complicated times, the religious searcher was confronted by relatively few choices ranging from Roman Catholicism and various Protestant churches to some old-line cults like Mormonism, Christian Science and Jehovah's Witnesses. Seldom could one find more unconventional practices such as witchcraft or Satan worship.

In 1955 a young evengelist preached that according to the Book of Revelation one day there would be widespread worship of the devil. Well-meaning elders of the church counselled him that if he did not stop preaching such foolishness he would ruin his credibility and damage his ministry. Today, over 30 years later, there is Satan worship in almost every city and town in the land. The town shere the evangelist had made his predictions is now the headquarters city of a satan cult.

What Is a Cult?

A cult is any religious movement that denies the truth about God as revealed in the Bible. Webster calls it a religion regarded as unorthodox or spurious. Only two religions have ever had the approval of God. One was the religion of the Jews as found in the Old Testament. The other is Christianity; revealed in the New Testament. All other religions are false and are deceptions of Satan. (See I Corinthians 10:14-21; Psalm 96:5; John 14:6.)

Cultic Error

A cult will be in error on one or more of the major concepts of the Bible. Here are examples:

1. The Nature of God. Mormonism teaches that God was the man Adam, who came to earth from another planet with his wife Eve to spawn the race of men on earth. Adam is our god. One day certain men will become gods and, like Adam, go and populate other worlds. Jehovah's Witnesses deny the Godhead (Trinity). Maharishi Mahesh Yogi, founder of the Transcendental Meditation movement denies the existence of a personal God.

2. The Nature of Jesus. The Bible shows Jesus is eternal and He is God. He is not a created being. The cultist may speak highly of Jesus; he may even seem to exalt Him. But if he denies Jesus is God, he is in error.

"In the beginning was the Word, and the Word was with God, and the Word was God. And the Word was made flesh, and dwelt among us." (John 1:1,14).

The Word is Jesus and Jesus is God. Isaiah saw the exalted Lord in the heavenly temple. No Christian questions that it is *God* whom he saw. Compare Isaiah 6:1 with John 12:38-41. Jesus is the Lord seen by Isaiah 700 years before His Bethlehem birth. Jesus said: "I and the Father are one." (John 10:30). Paul wrote: "For in Him dwelleth all the fullness of the Godhead bodily." (Colossians 2:9).

Strange Terminology

A man in Toronto had some very strange ideas. Attempting to find out what he believed, I asked, "Who is Jesus?"

He replied, "Jesus is God." So I asked for his definition of God.

"God is everything," he responded. "I am God, you are God, this building is God, the trees are God. Everything is God, therefore Jesus was God too." Of course this does not suffice.

Another cultist told me that Jesus, Lucifer and Jehovah are all gods. The New Process Church of Final Judgment teaches that Jehovah is getting senile. Jesus and his elder brother Lucifer have patched up their quarrel and are uniting forces to remove Jehovah from rulership of the universe. Charles Manson, mass murderer, claims to have been in the Process Church. He modified the doctrine and proclaimed himself both Jesus and Satan.

Other major areas of cultic error center on the nature of man, redemption and the authority of the Bible as God's exclusive revelation to man.

The Occult

The word *occult* literally means hidden or secret. We use it to describe cults that emphasize supernaturalism, magic or metaphysics. Not all cults are occult, but all occult groups are cults. Some cults are more philosophical and work in the area of the mind. Jehovah's Witnesses make no emphasis on present-day supernatural activity. Thus, the Witnesses are a cult, but not occult.

Examples of occult practices are witchcraft, fortune-telling, astrology, use of psychic appliances (voodoo dolls, a Ouija board, a pendulum, a crystal ball, hex candles etc.), aura balancing, psychic prophecy, tarot cards, psychic surgery and the like.

Cult Leaders

A concerned mother's definition of a cult was recently printed in a Seattle newspaper:

"I think of a cult as being a closed group directed by one person. Usually it is very totalitarian, has a very tight and closed structure and has a leader who is using the Bible and God for his own purpose, to benefit his pocket and put fear in his group.

Many cults center on the teaching of one strong personality. To his followers, the cult master is a messiah, a deliverer. He comes on the scene during a time of distress and trouble. He promises solutions to the world's and individual's problems. The extent of power that can be exerted by a cult leader was illustrated in the Jonestown massacre led by Jim Jones of the People's Temple. Nine hundred of his mentally and spiritually enslaved followers committed suicide (some murdered) at his command; so great was the power he wielded over his disciples of death.

The leader does not seem at all evil to his followers. He radiates virtue, peace and love. It doesn't seem to matter that he lives in luxury while his followers endure wretched conditions, suffer deprivations and go hungry. Even extreme and cruel punishment meted out to those guilty of a minor infraction of arbitrary rules is portrayed as an act of loving, fatherly concern. To the person drifting through life without a purpose, he offers easily understood, idealistic goals. He looks like a god or an angel of light."

"For such are false apostles, deceitful workers, transforming themselves into the apostles of Christ. And no marvel; *for Satan himself is transformed into an angel of light.* Therefore it is no great thing if his ministers also be transformed as the ministers of righteousness." (II Corinthians 11:13-15).

Exclusiveness

Some cults practice extreme methods; others do not. Rather than exercising mind control, some use a rationalistic or pseudo-intellectual approach. But all cults practice exclusiveness. They say, "We are the people who have the truth and there is none beside us. Everyone else is the enemy."

We admit that true Biblical Christianity also teaches exclusiveness. Jesus proclaimed that He alone is the way by which men can come to the Father. On the other hand, a wide variety of Christian denominations fully accept that others outside their ranks have had a real Christian experience. The concept of the uniqueness of Jesus and His redemption does not promote hatred of anyone. It promotes loving concern for the conversion of the lost, but not hostility toward them.

Some cults teach young people to hate their parents (Children of God, Moonies etc.), in direct contradiction to Scripture which instructs us to obey and honor our father and mother.

If you leave the cult you are considered a traitor against God. You have abandoned the only hope of salvation. You have defied the Lord. Another link is forged in the enslavement of a soul.

Witness Lee (The Local Church) states: "I am sorry to say that in today's Christianity so many Christians . . . are alienated from the life of God."

(*The Stream,* February 1977). Young members of the Local Church Cult can be seen wearing t-shirts with the slogan, "God Hates Christianity." According to Lee, God has abandoned all Christianity except the "Local Church."

Enlistment

The world is full of lonely, broken, confused people. Many are alienated from "normal" society. Disillusioned with modernistic Christianity, many have rejected the church. Our materialistic culture teaches young people how to make a living, but has little to say about the meaning of life. Multitudes are bent on a hedonistic (pleasure-seeking) life-style.

Sooner or later one faces sobering questions: "Who am I and what is the meaning of my life? What is the purpose of existence? Why is the world in such a mess? What can I do about it? How can I make my life count?" To the extent that the church fails to reach people with the true answers, a vacuum is formed and into that vacuum move Satan's deceivers with cultic answers and solutions.

Some are enlisted in cults by signing up for a seminar on self-improvement. This type of recruitment is used by such groups as Scientology, Transcendental Meditation, The Way International and Erhard Seminars Training, founded by Werner Erhard.

Others are enlisted when a cult missionary comes to the door with his message and literature. This is the major tactic of groups like Jehovah's Witnesses and the Mormons (Latter-Day Saints).

Fast-growing, youth-oriented cults use street-witnessing techniques that are highly effective. The Children of God, Hare Krishna and the Unification Church (Moonies) swell their ranks in this fashion. A young person is approached with literature, conversation and an invitation to come to a "party" or weekend retreat. He is told: "There is no charge and you will meet a lot of loving, concerned people. We really care about you and want you to find reality. You don't have to join us. Just come and see what our teacher has to say."

The meeting may be held in a house, a store-front or a camp-retreat. The "prospect" is surrounded by smiling, happy people. Never has he heard such enthusiastic singing and testifying. It seems so wholesome and innocent, if a bit simplistic.

The cults make a big promise: "How would you like to be set free from all fear, doubt and bondage; delivered from poverty, sickness and poor health; overflowing with life, vitality and zest; rescued from condemnation and self-contempt; cured of drug and sex abuse?'' (*Be a Winner,* distributed by The Way International). Who wouldn't be interested in such accomplishments?

The cult leader in person, or a trusted representative may be the speaker at the "retreat." The speech recounts the brokenness of the world, the failure of "the system," and the materialism of parents. His every statement is greeted with cheers, applause and shouted slogans. The teacher promises that solutions have been found; they have the answers. All they need is a band of dedicated followers to carry out the will of the master. "Enlist now and be a part of God's end-time program!''

The new contact then finds himself in a smaller "discussion" group. Scripture passages, strange doctrines and slogans are hammered at his tired mind by these ever-smiling, self-assured people. He begins to think, "They could be right. They sound so right - they must be right!" And the bondage is almost complete.

Cult Members are Made — Not Born

It is more natural to become a born-again Christian than to become a cultist. Many have become Christians just by reading the Bible. They have beliefs similiar to the mainstream of evangelical churches. But no one would become a Mormon, Christian Scientist or a Moonie just by reading the *Bible alone.* People become members of man-made cults only when the belief is superimposed on them through the non-Biblical teachings of the cult lord. Usually this superimposition is accomplished by those who are already in the cult.

Delivered Through the Word

Diane Devine was a highly positioned member of the Unification Church. She was handed a gospel tract consisting of Biblical quotations. After reading the tract she bought a New Testament. Solely by reading the Word of God, Diane decided the Unification Church was wrong. She had never had any church affiliation. Diane left the Unification Church because of the truth of the Bible. She is now a Spirit-filled believer. She made her exodus from obsession without any verbal witness, and she was never deprogrammed by anyone. The power of the Bible led her out of darkness into light.

Mind Control

Not to be taken lightly is the fact that many cults bring their subjects into a state of mental slavery through various brainwashing techniques. The Moonies, Children of God, Hare Krishna and the Way International are groups that practice such methods.

Many cult leaders have made a science of the art of controlling their subjects. The use of physical exhaustion; little sleep; repetitive propaganda drills; low-protein, high-carbohydrate diet; and isolation from all but dedicated members contribute to mental and spiritual enslavement. It is reported that members of one California-based cult seemingly lose their ability to read and concentrate.

The Local Church (Witness Lee) practices a technique called "Pray-reading" the Bible. Lee tells the members to turn off their minds and to shout out phrases of Scripture — it does not matter what the words are. Preaching, teaching and study are unimportant. One sad result of this strange methodology is that the participants are whipped up into a frenzy of hate against other segments of the body of Christ. Their vilification of the church goes beyond comprehension.

Devotees of cults often appear to be "spaced-out wearers of plastic smiles. Speak the true word of Christ to them and they may gaze over your shoulder, out of touch, unhearing, with mental blocks firmly in place — you are the enemy.

End-Time Spiritual Warfare

The rise and proliferation of false cults does not take the student of the Bible by surprise. Jesus, Peter, John and others warn of increased satanic deception in the last days, so that if it were possible the very elect should be deceived. This deception campaign employs human agents for its success. Hence, Jesus warned there would be false prophets and false teachers in the last days. (See Matthew 24:11, 24)

All Miracles Not of God

Just because a movement is supernatural or can produce miraculous accompaniments does not mean it is of God. There is more than one source of supernatural power. There is the power of God and also the power of Satan. John warns, "Beloved, believe not every spirit, but try the spirits whether they are of God: because many false prophets are gone out into the world." (I John 4:1)

Paul foresaw that:

"The time will come when they will not endure sound doctrine; but after their own lusts shall they heap to themselves teachers, having itching ears; and they shall turn away their ears from the truth, and shall be turned unto fables." (II Timothy 4:3-4)

We need not fear the cults, but we need to be informed to help others. God has given us many powerful tests of truth.

There is no way you could study all the cults, nor is there any reason to. The best defense against the cults is a good offense; that is, to be firmly grounded in the teaching of the Word of God so we are always "set for the defense of the gospel," and ready to "contend for the faith which was once delivered unto the saints." In this book, we will survey some of the prominent cultic movements to help equip you in the never-ending battle of truth versus error.

"He which hath begun a good work in you will perform it . . . in the defense and confirmation of the gospel." (Philippians 1:6-7)

Chapter 2

Network of Light

Since 1954 we have been preaching and teaching that there was a loosely knit world conspiracy, a so-called Network of Illuminists. We will give further clarification on the whole concept of conspiracy theories a bit later.

The Network of Light (New Age Movement) is nothing new. It dates to the fall of Lucifer, son of the morning. The Bible teaches that the ministers of Satan appear as *ANGELS OF LIGHT*.

One of the leading "lights" in the New Age Movement is an organization founded around 1923. It is very much alive and active today. Adam Weishaupt launched the Illuminati (light bearers) in 1776. Whether the Illumaniti has one special organization that is its organic descendant would be hard to prove; however we can be very sure that its philosophical torch bearers are represented by literally hundreds of organizations and individuals in many diverse realms. Proof of this claim will be offered in this chapter.

AN INTERESTING CORRESPONDENCE

I was talking with John E. Schroeder in the home of a friend in Saint Louis, Missouri, just a few nights ago. We were discussing the New Age Movement and the Network of Light concept. John is an ordained minister with the Missouri Lutheran Synod. After corresponding with him on different occasions since the early 1970's, I just learned that he is an enthusiastic Spirit filled (Charismatic) believer. I had felt that this was the case, but I am not prone to ask people for all the labels they wear. As best we can remember, our first contact came through a Rev. Aubushon, an Assemblies of God clergyman. It seems that John had been given a tape of one of my messages by Rev. Aubushon. Here is the text of a letter I received from Rev. Schroeder in 1973. The letter is dated September 1, 1973. It is interesting to note that this was the same period of time in which I had been given a vision by God relating to monumental spiritual warfare in the end times showing how the church might prevail over the forces of antichrist. For more information on this vision and the concept of end time victory for the church write and request a free packet of prayer and prophecy literature. Our address is: 304 E. Manchester; Springfield, MO 65807. (Send $2.00 for postage and handling).

Here is the letter from John Schroeder:

Dear David,
Rev. E. Aubushon of the Sparta, Illinois, Assembly of God Church heard me lecture recently at Red Bud, Illinois where I compared legitimate gifts bestowed by the Holy Spirit and occult practices involving other spiritual forces. The resources for the seminar are co-ordinated in the Students Packet for the course, "Faithfulness, Spiritual Gifts and the Occult", SPIRIT/TALK, Volume 2, Number 3, distributed by Concordia Publishing House in June 1972.

The discussion touched on a series of "prophetic utterances from 400 space prophets" who told of a new age and technology coming where space Brothers would enforce peace by apparent dictatorial means; and that a group internationally linked in a "Network of Light" espoused the second coming of a "Christ" who was to be followed without recourse to conscience even if "the Leader" commanded murder; and that all doctrines of Christian theology could be accepted by believers except "the doctrine of the Atonement because that is the only false doctrine. There is no evil, and all of us in his own way, is on the way to being God. Let this same mind-set be in you that was in Christ Jesus." Frankly, I admitted to the assembled Christians that, after my experience researching this course, my idea of the person and power of the anti-Christ changed appreciably. "We wrestle not against flesh and blood, but against principalities and powers and rulers of the darkness of this world" with implications — as pre-Christian Jews believed — that the principalities ruled some space kingdoms as evil emissaries of the negative spirit of the air.

Anyhow, you can obtain the Students Packet for about $1.75 from any Christian bookstore, or order it from Concordia Publishing House, 3558 South Jefferson Ave., St. Louis, MO 63118, or borrow it from a Missouri Snynod Lutheran Church which used the Mission Life series as high school discussion curriculum. Meanwhile, write me about "The Illuminati." The name is intriguing because leaders of The Network of Light claim publishing plants in the U.S. alone. Apparently all their affiliates have terms in them indicating "Light" but no one title is used consistently. "Illuminati" could be such an overriding designation. I would appreciate your sharing any facts you have and any theories which you have drawn from the facts.

Thanks for your help and blessings on your work for Christ."

John E. Schroeder

Later, on June 11, 1984, Rev. John Schroeder wrote the following:

Dear Brother Lewis,

Thank you for tracking me down by phone last week. I'm sure the Holy Spirit led you to call when you did.

Your concerns about updating my information about the Network of Light and correlating occult groups was both timely and essential. After your call, I was led to contact a scientist who — I learned — had been given technological revelations similar to those I received. He also was warned about the Network of Light, which led him to data about the Illuminati and the Trilateral Commission and possible demonic linkages internationally. The parallels should not seem astonishing, but they are. The last times are approaching and God warns through many channels.

Sincerely,
John Schroeder

NETWORK NO FANTASY

A number of Christian authors have written about the New Age Movement, the Network of Light. The John Ankerberg TV Show featured a debate on the subject. The most extensive works available are *HIDDEN DANGERS OF THE RAINBOW* by Constance Cumbey and *PEACE, PROSPERITY AND THE COMING HOLOCAUST* by Dave Hunt.

I am fully aware of the fact that Cumbey's work is attacked by many, principally because she labels some Christian, evangelical organizations as part of the New Age, or at least as having philosophy in common with the New Age groups. I do not know if Mrs. Cumbey interviewed any of these people before writing the book, but since she is trained as a lawyer, I would presume that she did. One of my good friends in Canada, an industrialist who is deeply involved in many Christian activities and organizations, takes strong exception to Cumbey's mention of World Vision in connection with the New Age Network of Light.

Apart from all of that, and even if the work is flawed (and I do not know that it is), nevertheless Constance Cumby has done a great service merely by getting the incredible discussion going on this subject. Perhaps it is the very fact that she is controversial that has opened the discussion up so widely. Christians who would have never known of the Network are now aware because of her.

I have never doubted that such a network existed. I have known and declared it since the early 1950's. Believe me it was difficult to get anyone to pay attention or take the matter seriously. A lot of Christians, even now, do not have the foggiest notion of what the New Agers have planned for us. What are the goals of the New Age devotees? First of all, they envision a one world government, a one world religion, a global community. Global 2000 is one of their catchy phrases which defines a time goal they have in mind for the establishment of a new world order. Why should this seem so fantastic to Bible believing Christians? Isn't this exactly what the Bible predicts for the day of the anticrist in the end of the age?

Of course some are influenced by a new wave of "charismatic" preachers and teachers who are denying the whole end time scenario of events. These new wave preachers declare that the "kingdom is now," there will be no rapture of the Church, nor will there be a literal millenium. One recently declared on national television that the Book of Revelation has nothing to do with end time events at all. Have you ever heard anything so absurd? Of course the kingdom is *now*. The kingdom of God is eternal. The Millenium is not the kingdom. But there will be a Millenium. It is a physical manifestation of the eternal kingdom of God. These preachers reject any literal interpretation of the Bible. Every man becomes a law unto himself in Biblical interpretation. The wildest fancies can be promoted in this manner. Perhaps these new wave "kingdom now" preachers are not consciously a part of the New Age Network of Light, but they certainly aid and abet the cause of the New Age.

We can easily establish that there is a New Age Network. We do not need to quote other Christian authors to do so. The New Agers themselves are becoming very open in their declarations of the existence and intentions of the movement.

NETWORKING

Networking is the title of a massive work by Jessica Lipnack and Jeffrey Stamps. This large paperback, which retails for $15.95, contains a listing of 1,526 organizations that are listed by their own choosing. Lipnack and Stamps sent out about 4,000 inquiries to organizations, inquiring if they would like to be included. No organization was included without choosing to be listed. The authors speak of creating "the universe we call another America." Believe me, the America they envision is not the America I want to live in. It is a socialist, occult America. Many of the listed organizations advocate world government as the solutions to our problems. Lipnack and Stamps describe the organizations listed as "network of networks. I have a feeling that the 1,526 organizations listed represent only the tip of the iceberg. Just this week we received a copy of *THE NEW AGE DIRECTORY* by Victoras Kulvinshas. It lists "3,700 entries in 45 categories . . ."

Some of the organizations listed by Lipnack and Stamps in *NETWORKING* are: Lucis Trust, Aquarian Age, Arms Control Asssociation, Planetary Citizens, World Constitution and Parliament Association, Futures Network, Findhorn Foundation, First Earth Battalion, Humanity Foundation, Institute for World Order, Kosmos Centre, L-5 Association, Office on Global Education, Planetary Society, Religion and Ethics Network, Triangles, Network of Light, World Federalists Association, World Union, World Peace Tax Fund, National Gay Task Force, Shambhala Publications, Sri Aurobindo's Action Center, T'ai Chi, Tayu Institute, etc. Numerous "Christian" organizations are listed along with the eastern swamis and occultists. Feminist groups, peace groups, nuke freezers, environmental concern groups, holistic health institutes and a host of other seemingly diverse groups seem to find something in common. It might be argued that not all of these groups are in agreement, nor do they have common goals. All I can say to that is that they chose to be listed in the book. I certainly would not choose to be listed in a publication without knowing what its purpose and philosophy was. I suppose it is possible that in some isolated instance a group could carelessly allow itself to be in such a listing. This, however, is an indictment against such a group. It would portray a dangerous laxness on the part of the leadership. It is my opinion that 99% of the groups listed here find themselves very comfortable in the company they have chosen. The publisher's back cover blurb explains, "Whether you're interested in bicycles, computers or day-care centers, solar energy, philosophy or meditation, you'll find your subject in *NETWORKING* . . . a direct route to whatever you need — or want — to know about the new age in which we live . . . *NETWORKING* . . . is a map of the modern world."

THE AQUARIAN CONSPIRACY

One of the most revealing publications is the book *THE AQUARIAN CONSPIRACY* by Marilyn Ferguson. The publisher's back cover promotion of this book states: "A great shuddering, irrevocable shift is overtaking us . . . It is a new mind — a turnabout in consciousness in critical numbers of individuals, a network powerful enough to bring about radical change in our culture. This network — the Aquarian Conspiracy — has already enlisted the minds, hearts and resources of some of our most advanced thinkers and steadily growing numbers from every corner of American society . . . Marylin Ferguson describes how this underground network is working to create a different kind of society based on a vastly enlarged concept of human potential.

The next chapter explores further into the Network of Light — the New Age Movement. We will examine some specific groups such as the Tara Foundation and the Lucis Trust.

Chapter 3

The New Christ

On April 25, 1982, one of the most massive religious advertising campaigns was launched. Full page advertisments appeared in the New York Times and other major newspapers across America and around the world. The estimated cost of this ad blitz was over a half million dollars. Here is the text of the advertisment which announced the appearance of a "New Christ."

THE WORLD HAS HAD ENOUGH
OF HUNGER, INJUSTICE, WAR.
IN ANSWER TO OUR CALL FOR HELP
AS WORLD TEACHER FOR ALL HUMANITY,

THE CHRIST IS NOW HERE

HOW WILL WE RECOGNIZE HIM?

Look for a modern man concerned with modern problems — political, economic, and social. Since July, 1977, the Christ has been emerging as a spokesman for a group or community in a well-known modern country. He is not a religious leader, but an educator in the broadest sense of the word — pointing the way out of our present crisis. We will recognize Him by His extraordinary spiritual potency, the universality of His viewpoint, and His love for all humanity. He comes not to judge but to aid and inspire.

WHO IS THE CHRIST?

Throughout history, humanity's evolution has been guided by a group of enlightened men, the Masters of Wisdom. They have remained largely in the remote desert and mountain places of earth, working mainly through their disciples who live openly in the world. This message of the Christ's reappearance has been given primarily by such a disciple trained for his task for over 20 years. At the center of this "Spiritual Hierarchy" stands the World Teacher, LORD MAITREYA, known by Christians as the CHRIST. And as Christians await the Second Coming, so the Jews await the MESSIAH, the Buddhists the FIFTH BUDDHA, the Moslems the IMAM MAHDI, and the Hindus await KRISHNA. These are all names for one individual. His presence in the world guarantees there will be no third World War.

WHAT IS HE SAYING?

"My task will be to show you how to live together peacefully as brothers. This is simpler than you imagine. My friends, for it requires only the acceptance of sharing.

"How can you be content with the modes within which you now live; when millions starve and die in squalor; when the rich parade their wealth before the poor; when each man is his neighbor's enemy; when no man trusts his brother?

"Allow me to show you the way forward into a simpler life where no man lacks; where no two days are alike; where the Joy of Brotherhood manifests through all men.

"Take your brother's need as the measure for your action and solve the problems of the world."

WHEN WILL WE SEE HIM?

He has not as yet declared His true status, and His location is known to only a few disciples. One of these has announced that soon the Christ will acknowledge His identity and within the next two months will speak to humanity through a worldwide television and radio broadcast. His message will be heard inwardly, telepathically, by all people in their own language. From that time, with His help, we will build a new world.

WITHOUT SHARING THERE CAN BE NO JUSTICE;
WITHOUT JUSTICE THERE CAN BE NO PEACE;
WITHOUT PEACE THERE CAN BE NO FUTURE.

These advertisements were sponsored by by the Tara Center of London and California. The front man and forerunner of the "New Christ" is Benjamin Creme, author of the book *THE REAPPEARANCE OF THE CHRIST AND THE MASTERS OF WISDOM.*

The New Christ, who once inhabited the body of Jesus has been in a state of meditation in the Himalayas for the past 1900+ years. He has now "Materialized a body," according to Creme's book. "He came into the world by aeroplane and so fulfilled the prophecy of 'coming in the clouds'. On July 8th, 1977, He descended from the Himalaya into the Indian sub-continent and went to one of the chief cities there . . on the 19th he entered a certain modern country by aeroplane. He is now an ordinary man in the world — an extraordinary, ordinary man." (From *THE REAPPEARANCE OF THE CHRIST AND THE MASTERS OF WISDOM* by Benjamin p. 55) Creme states that this New Christ will soon reveal himself as the World Teacher to guide us into *a new age* of sharing and justice for all. (Italics added to previous sentence.)

Of Jesus (not the New Christ) Creme says,

"In his next incarnation, as Apollonius to Tyana, Jesus became a Master. He lives now in a Syrian body which is some 600 years old, and has His base in Palestine. He has, in the last 2,000 years, worked in the closest relation to the Christ, saving His time and energy where possible, and has special work to do with the Christian Churches. He is one of the Masters who will very shortly return to outer work in the world, taking over the Throne of St. Peter, in Rome. He will seek to transform the Christian Churches, in so far as they are flexible enough to respond correctly to the new reality which the return of the Christ and the Masters will create." (From Reappearance of The Christ . . . p. 46.)

"The esoteric view, I submit, is more rational, more probable, and that is that Christ is a man. To my mind the Churches have over-emphasised the divinity of the Christ. He is divine, but in the way that you and I are divine." (p. 47)

Commenting on the nature of God, Benjamin Creme says the following on page 110 of the book we have been quoting:

"I would say that in a sense there is no such thing as God, God does not exist. And in another sense, there is nothing else but God — only God exists.

God to me — I am speaking intellectually now, from which angle one cannot know God, but since you have asked me for a definition (you have asked for the impossible, but I shall attempt it) — God is the sum total of all the laws, and all the energies governed by these laws, which make up the whole of the manifested and unmanifested universe — everything we know and see and hear and touch and everything we don't know or hear or see or touch, everywhere, in the totality of cosmos. Every manifested phenomenon is part of God. And the space between these manifested phenomena is God. So, in a very real sense, there isn't anything else. You are God, I am God. This microphone is God. This table is God. All is God. And because all is God, there is no God."

Bearing in mind what Creme says about Jesus, Christ and God (the Father) read these words from the writings of the apostle John who of all human beings was closest to our Lord Jesus Christ in His earthly sojourn:

"I have not written unto you because ye know not the truth, but because ye know it, and that no lie is of the truth.

Who is a liar but he that denieth that Jesus is the Christ? He is an-ti-christ, that denieth the Father and the Son." (I John 2:21-22)

One of the distinctive signs of the end of the church age is that there will be a proliferation of lying teachers and false Christs. Jesus said, "For there shall arise false Christs, and false prophets, and shall shew great signs and wonders; insomuch that, if it were possible, they shall deceive the very elect." (Matthew 24:24).

THE GREAT INVOCATION

Some time ago an attractive advertisment appeared in the Reader's Digest. At first glance it seems to be an innocent prayer. It is labeled "The Great Invocation." It calls for the second coming of Christ. Here is the test of "The Great Invocation:

> "From the point of light within the Mind of God
> Let light stream forth into the minds of men.
> Let Light descend on Earth.
> From the point of Love within the Heart of God
> Let love stream forth into the hearts of men.
> May Christ return to Earth.
> From the centre where the Will of God is known
> Let purpose guide the little wills of men—
> The purpose which the Masters know and serve.
> From the centre which we call the race of men
> Let the Plan of Love and Light work out
> And may it seal the door where evil dwells.

Let Light and Love and Power restore the Plan on Earth."

The invocation is followed with the following invitation to participation.

"The Great Invocation belongs to all humanity. Will you join the millions who daily use this prayer to invoke peace on earth? Become a co-worker in God's Plan, for only through humanity can the Plan work out. Card Copies (without charge) from: Lucis Trust, 866 United Nations Plaza, Suite 5667, New York, NY 10017-1888. Tel. (212) 421-1577."

According to Cumbey the Lucis Trust was organized in the early 1920's as the Lucifer Publishing Company. Later the name was changed to Lucis Trust. The group is also known as "The New Group of World Servers." The scope of the activities of this organization is indeed vast. The "Great Invocation" is printed and distributed in the following languages as of this writing, and the list is growing constantly:

Afrikaans, Arabic, Armenian, Catalan, Chinese, Czech, Danish, Dutch, Efik, Esperanto, Ewe, Fanti, Finnish, French, Ga, Gaelic (Irish), German, Greek, Guarani, Hindi, Hungarian, Ibo, Ibibio, Icelandic, Indonesian, Italian, Ivrit, Japanese, Korean, Latvian (Lettish), Lunya, Ruanda, Malay, Maori, Norwegian, Nyanga, Persian, Polish, Portuguese, Russian, Rumanian, Sesotho, Shangaan, Singhalese, Spanish, Swedish, Tamil, Tswana, Turkish, Urdu, Xhosa, Yugoslavic, and Zulu (Zula).

You may be sure that the Christ referred to in "The Great Invocation" is not the Christ known to Bible believing Christians. These cultists seem to recognize the one spiritual force that is able to defeat them. They decry Christian fundamentalists. A "World Goodwill Newsletter" (Lucis Trust) laments: "Even ten years ago it would have been difficult to forsee the resurgence of religious fundamentalism which has swept through some of the major world religions . . . In the United States for instance, the fields of both government and education are feeling the pressure of fundamentalist opinion. What is called 'Scientific Creationism' is being agressively promoted as an alternative to the scientifically accredited theory of evolution — Darwinism. Certain state legislatures are acquiescing and textbooks are being modified accordingly . . . Perhaps the most frightening and dangerous impact of fanatical fundamentalism upon the world community concerns the insidious effects of the 'apocalyptic vision.' In the United States particularly, many of the most fervent fundamentalists expect — perhaps even desire — the Biblically prophesied global cataclysm known as Armageddon. With nuclear holocaust an even more terrifying possibility, the political and social influence of many millions who sincerely believe in the scriptural necessity of the final holocaust can certainly be viewed as a substantial threat to world peace." I beg to disagree. It is not we who threaten world peace. It is the followers of the antichrist that will bring the cup of man's arrogant iniquity to the full and usher in the calamity of Armageddon. Christ's return to defeat the beast of Revelation is a program of rescue for the human race. According to Revelation Jesus returns to destroy the earth destroyers. It is no act of wanton slaughter; it is God's merciful intervention to prevent the antichrist from unleashing the fearful weapons of doom that would spell the end of all mankind. These cultists show an incredible lack of understanding of the scriptures. Or is it deliberate distortion? What in the world do they mean by the return of Christ? They are looking for a humanist, occult man-god. We look for the Son of God. He is not coming to destroy the world but to save it. We are not looking for the end of the world. We are looking for the beginning of the world. Jesus Christ our Lord, the Son of God, will return and there will be peace on this earth. Those who live faithfully for Him here and now will live in His peacable kingdom when it is visibly demonstrated on this planet.

The World Goodwill Newsletter reveals the depths of heresy of its proponents with this statement: "We are, in fact, divine beings . . . Fundamentally, we must believe in the divinity of Humanity."

The following is the text of a letter sent out to those on the mailing list of World Goodwill (Lucis Trust):

An Invitation to Men and Women of Goodwill

This is a time of preparation not only for a new civilization and culture in a new world order, but also for the coming of a spiritual dispensation.

Humanity is not following an uncharted course. There is a divine Plan in the cosmos of which we are a part. At the end of an age human resources and established institutions seem inadequate to meet world needs and problems. At such a time the advent of a Teacher, a spiritual leader or Avatar, is anticipated and invoked by the masses of humanity in all parts of the world.

This massed invocation reaches its highest point each year during the period of three great spiritual Festivals: at the great Western Festival of Easter; a month later at the Eastern Festival of Wesak, the Festival of the Buddha; and climaxes a month after that at World Invocation Day during the third Festival of the Christ which has the keynotes of goodwill and humanity.

World Invocation Day has three central features; first, the use of the Great Invocation, a world prayer which expresses truths central to all the major religions. Second: the spiritual cooperation of men and women of goodwill joining in a united act of invocation to divinity. Third: the distribution into human consciousness of the spiritual energies evoked during the Festivals of Easter and Wesak.

Today the reappearance of the world Teacher — the Christ-is expected by millions, not only by those of Christian faith but by those of every faith who expect the Avatar under other names — the Lord Maitreys, Krishna, Messiah, Imam Mahdi and the Bodhisattva.

Glamour and distortion surround this central fact of divine response to human need. This is inevitable but unimportant. The fact of transition into a new age is important. Preparation by men and women of Goodwill is needed to introduce new values for living, new standards of behaviour, new attitudes of non-separateness and cooperation, leading to right human relations and a world at peace. The coming world Teacher will be mainly concerned, not with the result of past error and inadequacy but with the requirements of a new world order and with the reorganization of the social structure.

Will you join in observing World Invocation Day through the united use of the Great Invocation, and will you join in making this day widely known?

WORLD GOODWILL

Conspiracy Theories

I have been studying conspiracy theories for the past 33 years — since I was seventeen years old. My findings indicate that no one can possibly understand the confusing data relating to world conspiracy theories except the Bible student. Only the eschatological element of the scriptures gives one the insight needed to tackle this complicated matter.

Secular students of conspiracy theories come up with diverse indentities of the would be rulers of the world. Some see a monolithic elitist organization with overwhelming powers. The great world conspiracy has been identified as the New Age-Network of Light, the Illuminati, the CFR and the Trilateral Commission, the Bilderbergers, Communism, Fascism, Free Masonry, the Mormons, the World Council of Churches, the Roman Church, and so on. One theory by Dr. Manly Hall reveals the conspiracy not as an evil thing but as the very salvation of humanity. This would agree with those in the Aquarian Conspiracy, The New Age, etc. Hall's concepts are found in a rare book, *The Secret Destiny of America*. Dr. Emmanuel Josephson claimed proof that the world conspirators are Christian fundamentalists plotting to overthrow the world. He projected this theory in his book *The Hidden Teachings of Jesus*.

Antichrist/Antichrists

The problem with the antichrist is that there are just too many candidates for the office! This comes as no surprise however, for John the apostle wrote:

"Little children, it is the last time: and as ye have heard that anti-christ shall come, even now are there many anti-christs; whereby we know that it is the last time." (I John 2:18)

There will be the final antichrist (singular), the very beast of Revelation. But there will be many antichrists (plural), who are the forerunners of the final son of perdition, the one who promotes man worship (II Thessalonians 2:3-4).

Michel Bertrand and Jean Angelini, two French scholars, see Weishaupt's Illuminati as a mere part of a larger and older conspiracy. Their book *The Occult and the Third Reich*, focuses on Hitler's part in the scheme. They cite Hitler himself as having said, "He who has seen in National Socialism only a political movement, has seen nothing."

The authors who write under the pen name Jean-Michel Angebert state, "Nazism is only the most recent outcropping of a militant neo-paganism locked in a death struggle which will go on to the end of time." The publisher's words on the back cover of the book state, "A member of the occult Thule group, Hitler sought to justify his theory of the 'supreme race' by acquiring the integral knowledge of good and evil. This knowledge, hidden in the past, contained the secret of the genesis of the world and, as Hitler believed, the justification for Nazi political theory, *The Occult and the Third Reich* shows that the Nazi movement was not an isolated aberration of modern Germany, but merely the most recent flowering of birth, and could well rise to power again." Applying this to Biblical prophecy would lead one to the conclusion that there are many human manifestations of the conspiracy of hell to dominate the world of God's creation.

"There Is A Conspiracy" — Ezekiel 22:25

So many contradictory attempts have been made to trace an actual organizational descent of the Illuminati that it is incorrect to speak of the conspiracy theory. One must speak of conspiracy theories.

There is one system of interpreting world events that does

not confuse and that is Bible prophecy. The Bible is 100 percent accurate in its predictions. It never fails. Theories rise and fall, but God's Word of the Almighty tells readers what is to come to pass in these days in which we are living as we approach the end of the age. The Bible mentions conspiracy over thirty times, as in Jeremiah 11:9: "And the Lord said unto me, A conspiracy is found among the men of Judah, and among the inhabitants of Jerusalem."

There have always been men of evil council who have conspired to rule over their fellow men. Today is no different, and as Christians approach the hour when the beast (antichrist) will rule this planet for a short season it is not surprising that many evil forces work to prepare for his coming. But the author of the plot to enslave humanity is Satan, not man. He uses men of diverse talents and positions that yield to him. There is no way that people or insignificant individuals could make war with a powerful politician or a super rich capitalist — even if we knew for sure he was in league with the devil. But there is a way Christians can wage effective warfare against the devil himself and cripple Satan's diabolical schemes for the oppression of God's people.

End Time Victory Program

The church is not programmed for defeat. The gates of hell shall not prevail against us. God will intervene when we invite Him to do so. Satan is trying to hinder the Church today through an attitude of defeatism. Some prophesy of coming oppression as if it were inevitable. Remember Nineveh? God's judgmental warning was given and the Ninevites responded. They repented and the judgment did not fall.

With the authority vested in us, Christians can battle the forces hell hurls against us. We can bind the spirit of antichrist. In a day when many in high places would like nothing better than to destroy the Church, we dare not give up in despair. The Holy Spirit, working through the Church is revealed in II Thessalonians 2 as the force that hinders the man of sin, the final antichrist from being revealed as long as the Church is in the world. If our very presence in the world is doing this, think what we can do if we consciously exert the believer's authority to bind the powers of hell (James 4:7).

Chapter 4

Mormonism

The whole history and credibility of Mormonism hinges on one spring morning in 1820; a day held sacred by millions of Mormons (Latterday Saints). That is the day when God supposedly, physically appeared to a 15 year-old boy, Joseph Smith, in a small town in the farmlands of upstate New York.

The purpose of the visit was for God to forbid Joseph to join any of the churches then in existence. He was told "That all their creeds were an abomination in His sight; that those professors (believers) were all corrupt" (Joseph Smith's *Pearl of Great Price*, 2:19). Thus assured that Christendom was doomed, Smith was not left to struggle amid the muck and mire of lost humanity. In 1823 a messenger "sent from the presence of God" appeared in brilliance before the youth.

Golden Plates

Quoting the Bible at great length, the angel Moroni, supposedly told of a book deposited in a nearby hillside, written on golden plates. This book reportedly contained "the fullness of the everlasting gospel," as delivered by the Saviour to the former inhabitants of this continent. Smith was allowed to uncover a stone box on the hill and view the contents, but it was not until September 1827 that he was supposedly allowed to remove the plates along with the "Urim and Thummim and breastplate." Seers used this paraphernalia in ancient times, and Smith would use them to divinely translate the reformed Egyptian characters into what is now known as "The Book of Mormon."

An Evangelical Press news release has just been issued, datelined Salt Lake City, stating the following:

"A letter from the first Mormon to Joseph Smith, the founder of Mormonism, may shed new light on the founding of that religion.

"In the letter from Martin Harris, which is being kept in a bank vault in Salt Lake City, the writer says that Smith found golden plates carrying a message from God with the help of a 'seer stone,' or a kind of magic looking glass. The letter also states that at first Smith was kept from getting to the plates by an 'old spirit' which had been transfigured from a white salamander.

"The most common explanation of how Joseph Smith got the plates is that an angel told him where to find them and that he translated them with the help of seer stones.

"When the existence of the 'white salamander letter' became known among Mormon historians last year, Mormon church officials refused to comment on the letter or to say if it is authentic. Protestants critical of Mormonism have said that this letter is an indication that the Book of Mormon is not of divine origin.

"The letter, dated October 23, 1830, was purchased by Salt Lake City businessman Steven F. Christensen, who is also a bishop of the Mormon church. He announced its existence last March, and said it would not be made public until its authenticity had been verified. Christensen expects to write a book on early Mormon history, and said this letter got him started on the project."

Holy Prophet

Anointed as God's prophet to usher in the last days, Joseph Smith took the mantle of authority with zeal. Building a tight cadre of devout believers, he began to compile a wide assortment of divine revelations. They ranged from the bestowing of blessings and gifts on the elect to the laws and ordinances of God's holy church. Luckily, God continued to speak in King James English and a second book of "new" holy scripture came into being. Originally published in 1830 as the *Book of Commandments,* it was revised and republished in

1835 under its present name, *The Doctrine and Covenants*. Since then it has been revised repeatedly.

In 1851 the church published a third new book of scripture, *The Pearl of Great Price*. It contains three sections: The "Book of Moses" which supposedly restores truths missing from the first five Books of the Bible. The "Book of Abraham" was a translation of a papyrus record Smith said he discovered in 1835. The third section consists of writings of Smith. It contains portions of his retranslation of the Bible, his personal history, and the articles of faith of the church.

Divine Authority

As all things were now believed to be restored to their original purpose by divine order, it was only proper that the authority of the "eternal priesthood" be reestablished. Smith taught that it was taken from the earth after the death of the apostles, and was gone for almost 1800 dark years.

No less than John the Baptist (resurrected) came to Joseph Smith and his friend Oliver Cowdery, in May 1829, to restore the Levitical priesthood and the ordinance of baptism. Commonly called the Aaronic or lesser priesthood, it deals only in temporal things of the church. It is considered the lower authority.

The higher Melchizedek priesthood was conferred on the two men a month later by the supposedly resurrected apostles Peter, James, and John. Therein was the fullness of God's holy power. Without it salvation was impossible, for the ordinances of salvation could not be performed without authority. With it, man could now act fully in God's stead— even to attaining godhood. (The authenticity of the material in this chapter is confirmed and partly furnished by Ed Decker, a former Melchizedek priest of the Mormon Church who is now a born-again Christian.)

On to Zion

The original presentation of the "new gospel" proclaimed that God would bring His people out of Babylon (the world) and set them apart in Zion (Independence, Missouri). (See *Doctrines and Convenants*, 45:71.) Not only did the followers of Smith separate from their past physically, but they were also set apart from society by the very nature of the "fullness of the everlasting gospel." The Book of Mormon teaches that anyone not belonging to the restored church belongs to the devil's church (I Nephi 14:10), and are all lost. Only the Mormons are in God's Church.

Smith's converts bought land and commodities, voted, and lived their lives exactly as the prophet instructed them. Walls of fear, bitterness, and strife rose between the Mormons and Babylon (the world). In this setting, Joseph Smith was to embark on two separate doctrinal paths that would lead the church into its deepest apostasy.

Other Gods

In April 1884, Smith revealed to the saints a new concept of the very nature of God.

"God himself was once as we are now and sits enthroned in yonder heavens. That is the great secret. We have imagined and supposed that God was God from all eternity. I will refute that idea." (Smith's Journal of Discourses, Vol. 6, 1884, p. 3.)

Not only did this world bring God into the reach of man's understanding, but as the prophet spoke a great excitement fell upon the people.

"You have got to learn to be Gods yourselves . . . the same as all Gods have done before you . . . namely by going from one small degree to another — from grace to grace, from exaltation to exaltation . . . to sit in glory as do all those who sit enthroned in everlasting power."

Smith taught that all men were literally gods in embryo. All could become gods, exactly as our God had done before us. If one is part of the true church and it's priesthood, with God's true prophet at the head; if one is found obedient and worthy; and if one's works of righteousness are acceptable to God in the judgment day, then one will be raised up to "Celestial Exaltation" and become a god or goddess. Each man will be given dominion over his own worlds without end; each with his many celestial wives.

Man is offered a chance to be everything that God is. No longer is man to rely on the cross of Calvary. Jesus' death gave us only resurrection to be judged for our own worthiness. Each man is now personally responsible for his own exaltation.

Polygamy

As Solomon "did evil in the sight of the Lord" (I Kings 11:6), 1,000 years before Christ, so Joseph Smith fell prey to the same lusts of the flesh. While his God had already spoken out in strong terms against polygamy as a crime to be equated with fornication (*Doctrines and Covenants* 101:6, 1835 edition), Smith is credited with having taken at least 27 women in plural marriage (Andrew Jensen, church historian, 1887).

When exposure and accusation, along with public outrage, burst forth in June 1844, Smith was ready. Not to be daunted by the prophet getting ahead of him, Smith's God had supposedly already spoken in 1843 and had made polygamy a "New and Everlasting Covenant and if ye abide not that covenant, then ye are damned." Not only did God save the day retroactively for Joseph Smith, but also polygamy would now be a sign of righteousness in God's eyes! The murmuring against Smith (in the Mormon Church) ceased as his followers struggled to be found worthy.

The End of an Era

The end came quickly and from within. In the midst of sending out missionaries, moving in new converts, building a temple for newly revealed "sacred" ceremonies for the elect, and becoming the most powerful voting block in the state of Illinois, Smith made a fatal mistake.

William Law, Smith's second counselor in the presidency of the church, a wealthy Canadian convert, was growing nervous over Smith's financial disasters. But, as discouraged as Law was over this, he was infuriated when the prophet tried to recruit his own wife, Jane, into his ever-growing "elect ladies" group!

In an effort to bring this infamy to an end, Law published charges against Smith in the *Nauvoo Expositor*. (Contrary to Smith's prophecy, discussed earlier, the church never made Independence, Missouri "Zion." Instead, the prophet settled in Nauvoo, Illinois.) Smith promptly had the press destroyed. Law then brought further charges against him from the safety of nearby Carthage, Illinois.

Within a few short, volatile weeks, Smith was brought to Carthage to stand trial. On June 27, 1844 a mob gathered and stormed the jail. Smith emptied his own six-shooter into the firing crowd, taking a toll; but within minutes he was dead — a martyr to his people.

West to Utah

In the midst of the confusion, Brigham Young rose to unite the majority of the saints and lead them away to the New Zion in Utah. Young was a benevolent dictator to his people. The era of new growth was not without pain, but he brought solidarity to the shaken church. Today Utah blooms in the desert. It is the Beehive State; meaning industrious living, the emblem of the Mormons. They settled and rested and built an empire.

The New Mormonism

It took Mormonism 117 years to gain its first million members, 16 years for its second million, 9 years for the third, and less than 5 years for the fourth! It is estimated that today the church grows at the rate of 1 million per year.

There are currently over 30,000 full-time missionaries on the field and the number grows daily. The church actively encourages every member to be a missionary. Wherever they are — in school, at home, or at work — they are busy proselyting. Over 150,000 saints are set apart for part-time mission.

The Corporation of the Presidency (a Mormon business cartel headed by the Mormon President) is among the 50 wealthiest corporations in the United States. Its investments range from food production to television, radio, and newspapers. The Mormons are a factor to be reckoned with in every corner of American life.

What Lies Ahead

The goal of Mormonism is simple. It is that the church shall become the kingdom of God on earth. The church will unite and dominate the whole world. It has an "end-time plan" that foresees a dangerous time when the United States Constitution will "hang by a thread" and will be saved only by the efforts of the Mormon church. The United States will become a Mormon theocracy. The nation will be ruled from the Mormon temple in the Washington D.C. area

Ed Decker, a former Melchizedek Priest in the church prior to his conversion, has shared this information with us. He tells of a group of Mormon men recently ordained as "gods". It is the destiny of one of these "gods" to find a person known as "the one mighty and strong," who is not presently a Mormon. This Mormon "god" will convert him and he will lead the Mormon church into the fullness of its power in the end times. The "one mighty and strong" is to bring together the unity of the world. That unity involves Mormon rulership. All the wealth and energies of the church are dedicated to fulfilling this destiny.

What's the Difference?

One could compare the Mormon end-time scheme to Biblical predictions of the millennial reign of Jesus and say, "What's the difference?" But to one who understands Bible prophecy there is all the difference in the World. Thousands of books and articles have been written about the many errors of Mormonism. The root of error lies, however, in the fact that they have gone after false gods. This has led them to a false Christ, a false salvation, and to self-exaltation.

The Nature of God

God has been specific about Himself and has not left any doubt as to His attitude toward those who follow after other gods (Deuteronomy 13:1-5). In Isaiah's prophecy the Lord declares: "I am he: before me there was no God formed, neither shall there be after me. I, even I, am the Lord; and beside me there is no savior" (Isaiah 43:10-11). Thus, God affirms His uniqueness.

No man shall ever become god or be His equal (Hebrews 6:13). The error of Mormonism is well described by the apostle Paul:

"Vain in their imaginations, . . . changed the glory of the

uncorruptible God into an image made like corruptible man, . . who changed the truth of God into a lie, and worshipped and served the creature more than the Creator'' (Romans 1:21, 23, 25).

I challenge the Mormon apologist to show a single Scripture Verse in the entire Bible that states that God is an exalted physical man who lived on some other planet, serving a god of his very own, and is a product of eternal progression. It just is not there. There is not one Scripture Verse that promises that we too shall be able to earn the same "godhood" as our God enjoys. And nowhere in the Word of God is polygamy the sign of God's righteousness.

Never does the Word of God indicate that the blood of Jesus is insufficient in paying all debts of sin and providing full redemption. Nowhere did Jesus ordain anyone to the "Holy Aaronic" or "Holy Melchizedek" priesthood. At no time did Jesus utilize any temple to perform secret rites or speak out blood oaths, as do the Mormons in temples today.

Many think Mormonism is just another form of Christianity that is about as different from orthodox Christianity as a Methodist is from a Lutheran. This is not the case. Mormonism is a totally different religion and has no common ground with Christianity whatsoever.

In a recent interview, Ed Decker told us:

"When I was a member of the Mormon church and involved in the Temple I believed that I could become a god when I died. I would be given many celestial wives and sent off to procreate spiritual children and have dominion over worlds, just like our God, Elohim had. I believed that God was once a man on another planet. God came to earth from that planet with one of his celestial wives, Eve, and was actually Adam."

Mormonism even teaches that man can evolve into beings higher than Jesus, who belongs to "the second kingdom." But to us Jesus is "Alpha and Omega, . . which is, and which was, and which is to come, the Almighty" (Revelation 1:8).

Chapter 5

Jehovah's Witnesses

Charles Taze "Pastor" Russell was born on February 16, 1852. He spent most of his early years in Pennsylvania managing men's furnishings stores and denying various doctrines of the Christian church. In 1870, at the age of 18, Russell organized a Bible class in Pittsburgh. From 1876 to 1878 Russell was the assistant editor of a small monthly magazine, but resigned in the midst of the controversy that developed over his arguments against the atoning work of Christ. Russell then founded "Zion's Watch Tower" in 1879.

The Watchtower's Hidden Roots

Russell was a prolific writer. In 1886, the first of a series of seven volumes titled *Studies in the Scriptures* was published. Russell wrote six of these. They show the mixture of the occult and out-of-context Scripture passages on which the Watchtower Society was founded. For example, volume 3 of this series has a number of diagrams of the Great Pyramid of Gizeh, which is near Cairo. In chapter 10, Russell writes:

"It acquires new interest to every Christian advanced in the study of God's Word; for it seems in a remarkable manner to teach, in harmony with all the prophets, an outline of the plan of God, past, present and future."

Russell then misuses verse after verse of the Bible; applying them to the Great Pyramid, then jumping to a number of conclusions. Among them are the ideas that the pyramid represents the plan of salvation (for which Jehovah's Witnesses believe they must work), and that the Great Tribulation would begin in 1914. Russell writes:

"Thus the Pyramid witnesses that the close of 1914 will be the beginning of the time of trouble such as was not since there was a nation — no, nor ever shall be afterward. And thus it will be noted that this 'Witness' fully corroborates the Bible testimony on this subject."

This was one of the first of a series of false prophecies published by the Watchtower Society. Of these, the following are typical. In 1918, in the publication titled *Millions Now Living Will Never Die*, Jehovah's Witnesses were taught:

"Therefore we may confidently expect that 1925 will mark the return of Abraham, Isaac, Jacob, and the faithful prophets of old, particularly those named by the Apostle in Hebrews 11, to the condition of human perfection."

In the October 8, 1968 edition of *Awake,* another generation of Jehovah's Witnesses was taught that the Lord provided an instrument for the most effective work in the remaining months before Armageddon. Russell established a system of false prophecies that has continued to the present. (See Deuteronomy 18:18-22.)

We Are the Only Ones

In 1908 the movement's headquarters moved to Brooklyn, New York, where it prospered. Although Russell died in 1916, many of his peculiar doctrines survive today. For example, Russell taught that it is impossible to understand God's plan of salvation apart from Russell's doctrines, and that to study the Bible alone, apart from his exclusivistic interpretations, is to walk in total darkness. Jehovah's Witnesses promote the same error today; substituting more recent Watchtower publications for Russell's writings.

Here Comes the Judge

Judge J.F. Rutherford took over when Russell died in 1916. Rutherford distinguished himself by frequent blistering attacks against "organized religion" and "Christendom" — a term that Jehovah's Witnesses use to mean every Christian organization not subservient to the Watchtower Society. This too survives to the present. Now (as then) the Watchtower Society strongly accuses "the devil's organization" (Christen dom and the clergy) of promoting every kind of evil. They publish wild statements like: "Had Christendom chosen to do so, she could have easily prevented World Wars I and II." Statements like these show that in addition to a very deep spiritual disorder, there was — and still is — a very deep psychological disorder among the Witnesses.

As Rutherford rose in power, any attempt to oppose him was treated as opposition to Jehovah God. When Rutherford denounced Russell's "pyramid prophecies" (after they had failed) a number of Russellites left the society. Rutherford promptly denounced them, threatening that they would "suffer destruction" if they did not repent and submit to Jehovah's will as expressed by the society.

Rutherford's ego approached the pinnacle when he declared, in effect, that he was the mouthpiece for Jehovah God. Rutherford's literary accomplishments dwarfed Russell's in sheer volume. By 1941 the judge had written over 100 books and pamphlets, which had been translated into 80 languages. Rutherford died in 1942.

The third president, Nathan Knorr, established the Gilead Missionary Training School in South Lansing, New York. He was a popular speaker, addressing over 250,000 Witnesses at Yankee Stadium. A later president, Fred Franz, admitted under oath, in 1954, that the Watchtower Society publishes errors which they must later correct, as time passes.

A Unique Bible Translation

The primary Jehovah's Witness Bible is called the *New World Translation* (NWT). It was prepared by persons of questionable scholarship at the Watchtower Society. They insist on remaining anonymous. The New World Translation systematically mistranslates nearly every verse that teaches the deity of Christ. The average Jehovah's Witness is entirely unaware of this, having been taught that the New World Translation is the finest translation available.

Carefully compare the following quotations from the New World Translation with the same passages in your own Bible:

1. John 1:1: "In [the] beginning the Word was, and the Word was with God, and the Word was a god."

2. Romans 9:5: ". . . to whom the forefathers belong and from whom Christ [sprang] according to the flesh: God, who is over all, be blessed forever. Amen."

3. Philippians 2:5-9: "Keep this mental attitude in you that was also in Christ Jesus, Who, although he was existing in God's form, gave no consideration to a seizure, namely, that he should be equal to God. No, but he emptied himself and took a slave's form and came to be in the likeness of men. More than that, when he found himself in fashion as a man, he humbled himself and became obedient as far as death, yes, death on a torture stake. For this very reason also God exalted him to a superior position and kindly gave him the name that is above every other name."

4. Hebrews 1:8-9: "But with reference to the Son: 'God is your throne forever, and [the] scepter of your kingdom is the scepter of uprightness. You loved righteousness, and you hated lawlessness. That is why God, your God, anointed you with [the] oil of exultation more than your partners.'"

These examples are typical; there are many other mistranslations in the New World Translation, all of which support the false Watchtower doctrines. Some Witnesses, having been made aware of the drastic differences between the many good translations available today and the New World Translation attempt to nullify the authority of other translations by claiming: "Those translations were made by trinitarians."

Watchtower Doctrines

Jehovah's Witnesses hold more false beliefs than can be covered in this chapter. One of the most damaging of their errors is exclusivism. This was expressed in *The Watchtower*, July 15, 1960:

"The Watchtower Bible and Tract Society, the governing body of Jehovah's Witnesses, identifies itself as God's sole collective channel for the flow of Biblical truth to men on earth in these last days."

Similar statements were published as early as 1917. Witnesses believe God speaks only through His organization, the Watchtower Society.

This tragedy is compounded by the fact that few Witnesses ever really study their own mistranslated Bible. If they did, they wouldn't be Jehovah's Witnesses. Instead, they study Watchtower literature that claims to be expressing the Bible's message. These publications claim that "Christendom" is corrupt and that Jesus Christ is not God, but the archangel Michael. They teach that only the Father is God and that the doctrine of the Trinity is an invention of the devil. According to this literature, Jesus Christ never rose bodily from the grave, but only as a "spirit creature," and He returned to earth in 1914 to be seen only by those who have "eyes of understanding."

You Only Think You Are Born Again

The Watchtower Society robs its victims of their God-given option to be born again, by teaching that it is "not necessary to be born again to have God's Spirit." They claim that only the 144,000 can be born again. Only this "little flock" has been chosen by Jehovah to live in heaven as the bride of Christ. Of course the 144,000 are all Jehovah's Witnesses. The very large remainder of Witnesses might survive the unspeakable horrors of the soon-coming Battle of Armageddon, but only if they do enough good works serving the Watchtower organization. Not all Witnesses will survive Armageddon, but those who do will inherit the earthly millennial kingdom.

The Holy Spirit

Watchtower doctrine denies the person and the deity of the Holy Spirit, teaching that He is merely "God's active force," like a mindless radio signal. Yet they teach that the devil and his demons are both spirits and persons, and correctly point out that the demons receive the worship of those who do not serve the true Jehovah God.

The New World Translation Refutes
Jehovah's Witnesses Doctrine

Watchtower doctrine cannot stand up under close examination in the light of the Word of God. But most Christians would never guess that the Watchtower heresies cannot even survive a close examination in the light of the mistranslated *New World Translation.* Jehovah's Witnesses are stunned when they are shown what their own Bibles teach about such vital matters as the deity of Christ.

An Assemblies of God minister has written a very carefully documented book on this subject, titled *Who's That Knocking at My Door?* This book uses only the *New World Translation* and other Watchtower documents to refute each of the many Watchtower arguments against the deity of Christ, to prove Jesus Christ is God the Son, and to prove the Holy Spirit is a Person and is Himself God. (Copies are available from Rev. Alex DiGenova, 13226 Chipman Glen Dr., Houston, Texas 77082.

God the Son in the New World Translation

The following proofs are taken from Alex DiGenova's book. If these proofs work in the *New World Translation* they will also work in your own reliable Bible translation.

The Witnesses frequently use John 1:1 in the *New World Translation* to "disprove" the deity of Christ. The Watchtower Society teaches that the Bible is to be viewed as [a] united whole," and that the "right explanation is always harmonious with the rest of God's Word." The *New World Translation's* rendering of John 1:1, "and the Word was a god," couldn't possibly be correct, because it is so completely out of harmony with many other correctly translated verses in the *New World Translation,* such as: Isaiah 43:10-11; 44:6-8; 45:5, 21, 22; 46:9; Psalms 18:31; 71:19; I Chronicles 17:20; Joel 2:27. These verses also refute the *New World Translation's* mistranslation of Philippians 2:5-6.

There are many proofs of the deity of Jesus in the *New World Translation.* In Revelation 21:6-7, God calls Himself "the beginning and the end," and in Revelation 22:13, "the first and the last." Isaiah 44:6 and 48:12-13 agree that Jehovah God is "the first and the last." But in Revelation 1:17-18 and 1:8 we learn that the first and the last "became dead," but now He lives forever and ever. This can only be a description of Jesus Christ.

In another proof, in Luke 4:6-8 in the *New World Translattion,* Christ commands Satan: "It is Jehovah your God you must worship, and it is to Him alone you must render sacred service." Yet, in Hebrews 1:6 in the *New World Translation*, Jehovah God the Father gives a command concerning His firstborn Son: "And let all God's angels worship Him."

Another interesting proof, not only of the deity of Christ but also of the three Persons of the Godhead working in perfect triunity, centers on who raised Jesus from the dead. According to the *New World Translation*, the Father did it (I Thessalonians 1:9-10), Jesus Himself did it (John 2:19-22), the Spirit of God did it (Romans 8:11), and God Himself did it (Acts 17:30-31; Romans 10:9). (References are from the 1971 revision of the *New World Translation* of the Watchtower Society.)

Further Embarrassment for the Watchtower

The Watchtower Society's insistence that Jesus was resurrected as a "spirit creature" is refuted in the *New World Translation* by John 2:19-22; 20:27-28; and Luke 24:39. Jesus Christ ascended bodily into heaven and will return the same way, for all to see, according to the *New World Translation*. (See Matthew 24:30; Luke 21:27; Acts 1:9-11; and Revelation 1:7.)

The *New World Translation* is quite clear on the matter that only those who are born again can ever hope to see the kingdom of God (John 3:3), and that only those who have Christ's Spirit belong to God (Romans 8:9-11). The *New World Translation* teaches that it is absurd to claim that only 144,000 can be saved (Acts 13:47; Romans 1:16; I Corinthians 1:18; I John 2:2; Revelation 7:9-10).

The New World Translation and the Holy Spirit

According to the *New World Translation*, the Holy Spirit is God (Acts 5:1-11). That He is a Person is without question, because in the *New World Translation* people treat Him as a person. They obey Him (Acts 10:19-23; 11:12). They lie to Him (Acts 5:3). They grieve Him (Ephesians 4:30). They resist Him (Acts 7:51). They hurt Him (Isaiah 63:10). They reverence Him (Psalm 51:11). They can blaspheme Him (Matthew 12:31-32). He can be outraged (Hebrews 10:29).

There is no resemblance between the message preached by the Watchtower Society of Jehovah's Witnesses and the God-honoring, Christ-glorifying message found in your Bible.

Chapter 6

Christian Science

Mary Ann Morse Baker, better known as Mary Baker Eddy, was born on July 16, 1821 in Bow, New Hampshire, the seventh child of a sharp-tempered, devout Calvinist and his serene wife. At the age of 12 Mary was already denying the faith of her father. She was a sickly child; missing a good deal of schooling because of her poor health.

Mary was largely self-educated. She was given to long periods of depression and outbursts of extreme temper. She argued bitterly with her father against his strong beliefs in such matters as the wrath of God on sinners, a final judgment day, and eternal punishment for sinners. Mary would eventually reject all historical Christian teaching. She grew up a bitter, sickly young woman.

In 1843, at age 22, Mary was married to George Washington Glover. Even though he was to be the first of three husbands, he was probably the only one she really loved. When they had been married only 7 months, George died from yellow fever. This devastated Mary, who was pregnant at the time. She became highly unstable, an emotional invalid. As the October 30, 1906 and May 8, 1907 editions of the New York World reported, she began using morphine as a medication from time to time, and continued to do so throughout her life. Her child was born in 1845. She named him George W. Glover, Jr.

Almost 10 years to the day after her first husband died, Mary married a handsome dentist, Dr. Daniel Patterson. This marriage, too, ended in disaster. Patterson apparently was not fond of Mary's chronic sicknesses, spells of hysteria, and frequent bad temper. Some say that he left Mary, after years of unfaithfulness, for another woman. Others say he left because he could stand her no longer. After 13 years the Pattersons separated and then divorced, with Mary bringing charges of adultery against him.

Phineas the Founding Father

Before this separation took place Mary met the man who turned her whole unfortunate life around. In 1862 at the International Hotel in Portland, Maine, Phineas P. Quimby "healed Mary Baker Glover Patterson of what she called "spinal inflamation." If Mary could correctly be called the "Mother of Christian Science," then "Doctor" P.P. Quimby was it's father. He was 60 at the time.

Phineas P. Quimby was one of a number of "healers" who had discovered that certain people could be healed by a liberal dose of psychology and hypnotism. Quimby had, at various times, referred to his technique of mental healing as "The Science of Man," "The Science of Christ," and "Christian Science," long before Mary adopted these names as her own.

All Quimby did on that fateful day was to put his hands in water, rub Mary's head, and put her to sleep. When she awoke, all "sickness" was gone. Mary became a faithful disciple, dedicating the next several years of her life to spreading the gospel of Quimbyism. From 1864 to 1870 Mary went from door to door, teaching the Quimby "science of healing." She used a copy of a Quimby manuscript that had been in existence at least 9 months before she met Quimby; she had her students copy it while she guarded it jealously.

Later, Mary plagiarized extensively from this and other Quimby manuscripts (as well as from other sources) to write her book *Science and Health*. Christian Scientists deny this, however, insisting that Mary Baker Eddy was the sole discoverer and founder of their religion.

After Three Days She Arose

Mary was convinced that Quimby had rediscovered the healing methods of Jesus. Quimby died in January 1866. The following month Mary slipped on an icy sidewalk and was painfully injured. Mary claimed her doctor had declared her injury to be fatal. But, after suffering for 3 days, she read about the healing of the paralytic man by Jesus (Matthew 9:2-8). At that point the "truth" dawned on her and she arose, fully cured.

Mary's doctor, however, completely disagreed. In an affidavit dated August 13, 1904, Dr. A.M. Cushing swore that he had never pronounced her fatally injured, and that she had never told him anything about a "miraculous healing."

Regardless, Mary thereafter insisted that Christian Science was born on the date of her healing, which also was the date of the second coming of Christ. The return of Christ was a spiritual event, invisible to the naked eye except as seen in the birth of Christian Science. What actually was born on that date was a false religious system that would make Mary Baker Eddy a millionaire.

The New Movement

Mary (still Mrs. Patterson at the time) now launched her career as a teacher of healers-to-be. One source reported that by 1870 she was charging $300 for 12 lessons. She and Dr. Patterson had since gone their separate ways, and Mary was beginning to amass a fortune by speculating on the sicknesses of others. She never gave a penny to charity, in spite of her followers' repeated claims that she was "generous" and "kind."

In 1875 she bought a house in Lynn, Massachusetts, where, with eight followers, she formed an association called "The Christian Scientists." She finished working on the manuscript for the first edition of *Science and Health,* which was largely a collection of plagiarisms. Even though her manuscript was edited by a retired Unitarian minister, no publisher would touch it. Three of her associates financed its publishing.

In 1877, Mary Baker Glover Patterson married Asa G. Eddy. Although she was 56 at the time, she allowed the wedding certificate to indicate her age as 40. Her husband was a meek and obedient individual, and a student of Christian Science. In fact, he was the first to be granted the title "Christian Science practitioner." He was talented at business, and saw to it that Mary's second edition of *Science and Health* was profitable.

That same year the name of Mary's movement was changed to "Christian Science Association," and later, to "Christian Science Church." Largely because of a rebellion of many of her students, "Mother Eddy" (she was now 61) moved from Lynn to Boston. There she founded "The Massachusetts Metaphysical College." Sources state that she taught some 4,000 students at a cost of $300 per student over a period of 8 years.

Physician, Heal Thy Husband

Having uttered the statement: "Mrs. Eddy could not be pleased by God Almighty Himself," Asa G. Eddy died. His wife, who claimed to be able to heal all manner of illnesses, was utterly unable to do anything about it. A post-mortem examination proved he had died of heart disease. But Mrs. Eddy announced the cause of death as "mesmeric poison" (in other words, mentally administered poison). She cited Dr. C.J. Eastman as the attending physician who supported her claims. But "Dr." Eastman was a quack. He had no medical degree, and later served a 5-year prison term for running an illegal abortion mill.

Even "Mother" Eddy's preposterous claims about "mental poison" have become a doctrine. Also known as "Mental malpractice" and "malicious animal magnetism" (MAM), it has today become the demon against which Christian Scientists must continually defend themselves. Of course, when "Mother" Eddy herself died, MAM was the villain, even though pneumonia was the cause.

Physician, Heal Others

Perhaps it was MAM that caused "Mother" Eddy's ego to blossom as it did. On December 19, 1898, she wrote to the *New York Sun:*

"I challenge the world to disprove what I hereby declare. After my discovery of Christian Science I healed consumption in the last stages that the M.D.'s . . . declared incurable. . . . I healed malignant tubercular diphtheria and carious bones that could be dented by the finger. . . . I have healed, at one visit, a cancer that had eaten the flesh of the neck as to expose the jugular vein so that it stood out like a cord."

A prominent Cincinnati physician, Dr. Charles A.L. Reed, promptly accepted her challenge. In his letter published by the *New York Sun* on January 1, 1899, he offered to make all necessary arrangements for Mrs. Eddy to heal identical cases then being treated at Bellevue Hospital. Of course, "Mother" never accepted his offer; it would have been the death of her movement and her income.

The president of the Christian Science Mother Church in Boston, Mr. Alfred Farlow, testified, under oath in court, that he did not know of any ailment ever healed by Mrs. Eddy in her entire life, except "stiff leg." Mr. Farlow was also chairman of the Publication Committee of the Christian Science Church at the time, and certainly was in a position to know the facts about "Mother" Eddy.

Physician, Heal Thyself

The facts show that Mary Baker Eddy was never able to heal as she claimed, and was unwilling to put her "powers" to an open test. In fact, she used the services of a medical doctor in her later years, even continuing her use of morphine as a pain killer. But her easy promises of divine health without the Divine Healer, Jesus Christ, continued to attract converts, and the cult grew. The rest of "Mother" Eddy's life was a continual gathering of wealth while constantly suffering from "enemy magnetism."

Mary Baker Eddy died at the age of 89 on December 3, 1910. In accordance with her last wishes, her associates announced that she had been "mentally murdered." She left behind a personal fortune of over $3 million, and a huge organization that claims divine inspiration for her voluminous writings and deifies her memory.

Mother's "Divine" Beliefs

Mary Baker Eddy and the Christian Science Church deny all major doctrines of the historical Christian Church. Mary's book, *Science and Health*, speaks of the hundreds of thousands of mistakes in the Bible, and calls Genesis 2:7 a lie. "Mother" Eddy's writings deny the Trinity, and go to great lengths to deny Jesus Christ. Mrs. Eddy denies the lordship and deity of Christ as well as Hs atonement and resurrection. She even denies that Jesus is the Christ.

The "God" of Christian Science is very much like the "God" of Hinduism — all-in-all, all good, all loving, the infinite Mind (or Spirit). Because "God" is all of these, everything that is not Spirit does not exist. Matter does not exist because matter is not Spirit. If matter doesn't exist then neither do disease, sin, and death. Only that which is good exists. God and man are one; everyone is a part of God. Therefore, there is no need for salvation, resurrection, or final judgment — none of which exists anyway.

The Christian Science Headache

It is not necessary to consult the Bible to see that there are gross contradictions within Christian Science doctrines. For example, how can Christian Scientists call themselves "Christian" and deny the Christ? On the other hand, science deals with matter. How can they call themselves "Scientists" and deny that matter exists? If matter doesn't exist, then disease doesn't exist, as they frequently assert. How, then, can Christian Science practitioners heal that which doesn't exist?

If sin doesn't exist, why did "Mother" Eddy spend her final years behind locked doors in fear of MAM, and why do her followers continuously ward off MAM attacks? If there is no death, why do all people, without exception, die? If sin is merely an "illusion," what do Christian Scientists do, once they have died in their sins?

It isn't easy to enter a stately Christian Science Church and believe that the chair supporting you is not real. It is hard to refuse needed medical help that could save your life. Nor is it easy to watch a loved one die a lingering death under the "care" of a Christian Science practitioner. It is difficult to live in a world of sicknesses, sorrows, sufferings, injustices, and enormous evils, all the while convincing yourself it is all merely "an error of the mental mind." It is extremely difficult to grow old in constant fear of "enemy magnetism," or MAM. But such is the bondage that results from trusting an obvious lie.

Contemporary Quackery

The eminent French scientist, Stephen Paget, studied the healing methods of Christian Science practitioners, and then stated:

"They bully dying women, and let babies die in pain; let cases of paralysis tumble about and hurt themselves . . . watch, day after day, while a man or woman bleeds to death; compel them who should be kept still to take exercise, and withhold from all cases of cancer all hope of cure."

Today, Christian Science practitioners continue to feed on the sicknesses and sufferings of others.

There are some cases of Christian Science healings that seem to be verified. Because of these, Christian Science has spread, in spite of the incredible contradictions of Mrs. Eddy's doctrines. Indeed, in several states Blue Cross and Blue Shield (as well as hundreds of other insurance companies) now cover the "cure" provided by Christian Science practitioners who have the same status as ordained ministers, not medical doctors. The typical practitioner charges a nominal daily fee to "pray" for the afflicted, and may or may not make house calls. Many of them prefer to provide their services by telephone.

How Can It Work?

Jesus healed a woman who had been bound by Satan for 18 years (Luke 13:11-16). If Satan can bind people he can also set them free if it serves his deceptive purposes. Those cases of Christian Science healings that have been verified are a direct fulfillment of Matthew 7:15-23. Healing is not always a sign of the favor of God; in fact, it never is when it comes through those who deny the very Christ in whose name they claim to heal. God works only to the glory of Jesus and in perfect accord with the doctrines of the Bible.

The Christian Science Church stands in full opposition to the authority of the Bible. It is in contradiction to Isaiah 40:8; Matthew 24:35; Mark 13:31; Luke 21:33; John 10:35, 17:17; II Timothy 3:16. "Mother" Eddy may deny that Jesus is the Christ, but God the Father disagrees (Matthew 16:16-17). The deity of Jesus is taught in many places (Isaiah 9:6; John 1:1-3, 14; Romans 9:5; Colossians 2:9; I Timothy 3:16; Titus 2:13; Hebrews 1:5-10; I John 5:20).

Mrs. Eddy's claim that the second coming of Christ has already occurred is absurd in view of present world conditions and Acts 3:20-21. When the King returns, it will be for all to see (Matthew 24:30; Revelation 1:7, 19:11-16). It is absurd to deny the existence of sin (Romans 3:23, 6:23; I John 1:10, 3:4, 5:17). The Christian Scientist's denial of the existence of matter, sickness, and death is too ridiculous for further comment.

Divine Healing Is Real

There is healing for God's children. There is only one Healer — Jesus. Christians are to call for the elders of the church for prayer when sick, and expect to be healed (James 5:14-15). Divine healing is taught throughout the Bible. The operation of the true gift of healing (ICorinthians 12:9) always glorifies Jesus, not man (Psalm 103:1-3).

Gifts of healing are manifestations of the love and mercy of a real, personal God who grants healing on the basis of His grace, not on the basis of our mental exercises or good works (Psalm 103:10-14). We must be careful that in rejecting the pseudo-healing of Christian Science we do not reject God's healing.

Chapter 7

Man-Centered Cults

The temptation to elevate man to the position of God has its roots in antiquity. It was woven into the temptation of Eve with the words, "Ye shall be as gods" (Genesis 3:5). (Also see Isaiah 47:10.) Man-centered religions range from outright humanism to self-help cults like EST (Erhard Seminars Training). Some of the cults discussed in this chapter are pantheistic (everything is god); some claim a god concept but, nevertheless, are man-centered.

Humanism

Humanism is the philosophy affirming that man is the supreme reality. There is no god but man. The only salvation is that which man creates through his own efforts. Jehovah did not create man in His image as the Bible says, rather primitive man created a "god" in the image of man to explain the mysteries of a universe he could not comprehend. With the advent of modern science this god is no longer needed. Man alone is deity.

In *Religion Without Revelation* (Westport, CT: Greenwood Press, Inc., 1979), Julian Huxley says that he intends to prove that "religion of the highest and fullest character can co-exist with a complete absence of belief in revelation . . . [or] a personal god."

A Presbyterian minister, Dr. John H. Boyd, writes: "Those who can see the infinite reach of themselves can see God." He further says: "Man is limited because he does not believe in his own divinity."

In his book, *The New Theology*, Dr. R.J. Campbell writes: "God is continually incarnating Himself in human life."

A past president of Union Theological Seminary, Dr. M.C. Griffert, wrote in *The Rise of Modern Religious Ideas:* "Divine and human are recognized as truly one."

Over 100 years ago, Horatius Bonar wrote prophetically of the coming humanism:

> The Christ of God is now no more;
> The Christ of man now sits supreme;
> The cross is part of mythic lore,
> The resurrection morn a dream.
> Not faith in God, but faith in man,
> Is pilot now, and sail, and oar;
> The creeds are shrivelled, cold, and wan;
> The Christ that has been is no more.

Humanism is an unnatural thing. Nature itself teaches us there is a God (Romans 1:20). Humanists and atheists declare a belief that even demons dare not proclaim: "The devils also believe and tremble" (James 2:19).

Organized Humanism

Later roots of humanism are found in Confucianism and Greek and Roman philosophy. However, it did not become an organized movement until 1933, with the first humanist manifesto. The movement now claims about 3 million members, of which about 250,000 are in the United States. The American Humanist Society and the American Ethical Union are representative groups in the humanist movement.

A recent humanist convention in New York produced the second humanist manifesto. It declares: "No deity will save us, we must save ourselves." The signers included luminaries from the fields of politics, religion, literature, and social sciences. It continues:

"Promises of immortal salvation or fear of eternal damnation are both illusory and harmful. They distract humans from present concerns, from self-actualization, and from rectifying social injustices."

The manifesto also calls for a world government as the solution to many of mankind's ills.

Modernism

The apostate condition of great segments of Protestant Christianity has contributed to the growth of a multitude of modern cult movements.

The German school of higher criticism in the last century gave rise to the modernism of this century. Paul warned that the day would come when men would not endure sound doctrine (II Timothy 4:3). The many manifestations of modernism have one thing in common: the supernatural character of the Bible and the divine nature of Jesus are denied. The miracles of the Bible are explained away in humanistic terms.

Modernism gives rise to a host of evils, such as situation ethics or the "new morality," which is neither new nor moral (Isaiah 5:20). It is the father of the "God is dead" theology. Modernists can be classed as wolves in sheep's clothing. They use the church for its own destruction. An annual report of the American Association for the Advancement of Atheism stated:

"The liberals (modernists) are saving the ship of Christianity by throwing her cargo overboard. With what zeal the whole crew of rescuers toss out the virgin birth, the atonement, and the resurrection! How long will men sail the seas in an empty ship? They will go ashore and enjoy life with the atheists. We welcome the aid of the liberals and pledge them our fullest cooperation in ridding the world of any serious acceptance of Christian theology" (W.A. Criswell, *In Defense Of The Faith* [Grand Rapids: Zondervan Publishing House, 1967]).

When the church throws out the supernatural, miracles, and the divine nature of Jesus, people turn to the occult. If the church denies the Bible is God's message, then people look elsewhere for guidance, purpose, and strength. Modernism turns the church into a humanist cult. Modernism is not Christianity. It is a denial of Biblical Christianity. What a tragedy when the clergy are guilty of acts of apostasy instead of working the acts of the apostles!

Erhard Seminars Training

EST was founded in 1971 by Werner Erhard (formerly Jack Rosenberg), who had previously been involved in Scientology, mind dynamics, Silva mind control, yoga, hypnotism, and Zen Buddhism. EST is an intensive 60-hour training course designed to restructure a person's concept of reality through Erhard's mind-assaulting indoctrination. At the beginning of 1979, EST claimed 160,000 graduates.

John Denver, EST graduate, wrote a song about EST, "Looking for Space," and one of his albums is dedicated to Erhard. The singer also wrote the theme song for EST's film promoting the "hunger project." EST was praised before a TV audience of 36 million (the Emmy Awards) by Valerie Harper (Rhoda).

Destruction of Values

EST is designed to destroy a person's attitudes and life philosophy, including religious belief. Tension builds as participants are abused, told they are useless, and harassed with vulgarity and insults. Many would not attend if they realized in advance the trauma they would be pushed into. Participants are told to keep the nature of the seminar secret. The very intensity of the experience causes some to become dependent on EST. Authoritarianism combined with common sense psychology is overwhelming. Here is an example of brainwashing for willing victims.

Reaction varies. Some scream for help, others weep quietly; some vomit, others become mentally ill. The participant is told that he alone is god and is totally responsible for his present condition. The only help comes from himself, but EST provides the means to this self-salvation. One can see how this would appeal to middle and upper class Americans. If one is responsible for his own universe and has a degree of success, this success becomes a security and assurance factor — it is self-worship.

The Hunger Project

Since every man is responsible for his own circumstances and causes his own problems, EST teaches that charity is unnecessary. The EST World Hunger Project, therefore, seems to be a contradiction. It has raised vast sums of money. Critics of EST make the accusation that more of this money has gone into EST coffers than to feed the hungry.

The frightening thing about EST is the degree to which it has been accepted even by the public education system. A number of federally funded EST's have been provided for both children and teachers. Almost 10 percent of the teachers in the San Francisco area are EST graduates. Erhard states: "The real thrust and goal of EST is to put it in education" (*East-West Journal,* September 1974).

A basic EST doctrine is that man is his own god and each man causes all the events that affect him. But the Bible teaches: "He that cometh to God must believe that He is, and that He is a rewarder of them that diligently seek Him" (Hebrews 11:6).

Scientology

Ron Hubbard, a science fiction writer, launched Scientology not as a religion, but as a self-help therapy system known as "Dianetics." The Sussex, England, based organization was renamed Scientology in the 1950's and reformed as a religion. Critics claim this was to avoid taxation. Even after the change, it still has more in common with psychoanalysis and science fiction than with religion.

Scientology claims to be the "true way" and has the technology to make it accessible. The process entails awakening awareness of past lives in order to arrive at self-knowledge, awakening the primordial god within, and then attaining total godhood. Hence, man becomes his own god.

Man is basically good and consists of body, soul, and "thetan." The thetan is a kind of deified spirit that wants to control the body through the mind. The ultimate goal is to allow one's thetan to have absolute control of the mind; "to be clear." One must get rid of "engrams" (hang-ups, inhibitions, tensions, etc.). which warp the mind. Members are constantly in the process of getting rid of engrams.

Psychological tests are administered to discover problem areas. Scientology teachers (auditors) then make use of an "E-meter" to discover engrams. The auditor endeavors to help the member become "clear" or engram free. Scientology is not for the poor; it has nothing that is free. Each session costs from $15 to $60.

Hubbard says Jesus was a man who achieved a "state of clear" but never reached the highest state of "operating thetan."

The Unity School of Christianity

Some years ago I asked a student of Unity, "Who is God?" He replied, "God is everything." This aptly expresses the Unity concept of God — pantheism — the teaching that God is nonpersonal and permeates everything.

In 1886, Charles and Myrtle Fillmore attended a lecture by Dr. Eugene B. Weeks,. a lecturer for the Illinois Metaphysical College (founded by Emma Hopkins, an associate of Mary Baker Eddy, founder of Christian Science). Both Charles and Myrtle claim to have received healing through the teaching of Weeks. Desiring to share the good news, they published the first edition of *Modern Thought* in 1889. In 1891 the name *Unity* was adopted for their movement.

For 30 years, the Fillmores would not issue a statement of belief because they hated dogma. When a statement of faith was finally published, Fillmore said: "We are hereby giving warning that we shall not be bound by this tentative statement of what Unity believes. We may change our mind tomorrow." Note that the Bible says: "A double-minded man is unstable in all his ways" (James 1:8).

Rapid growth of Unity has taken place under the leadership of Fillmore's two sons, Lowell and Rickert. Unity emphasizes health and prosperity. They believe in the unity of the soul with God, the unity of all life, the unity of all religions, and the unity of spirit, soul, and body. Reincarnation is also taught.

Regardless of the lovely sentiments presented in Unity literature, to join Unity demands a renunciation of every major teaching of Christianity. Unity teaches that the Bible is not divine revelation, but merely a fallible human witness to revelation. Unity clearly says: "There is no sin, sickness, or death." (*Unity* Vol. 47, No. 5, P. 403) (Cited by Walter Martin, *Rise of the Cults* [Santa Ana, CA: Vision House, 1977]).

The Bible says: "If we say we have no sin, we decieve ourselves, and the truth is not in us" (I John 1:8). "The wages of sin is death." (Romans 6:23). Since Unity does not believe in the reality of sin, there is no need for the redemptive work of Christ. And Jesus is not God, but a mere human who demonstrated the "Christ ideal" that is in all of us. Jesus' death was not for atonement, but to demonstrate the power of mind over matter.

Measure of Truth

If the Bible is not the standard by which truth is determined, there is no standard. The Word of God withstands every criticism and every blow against its integrity and authority. Jesus said: "Thy word is truth" (John 17:17). (See also John 10:35; 12:44-50.) Can we hold a lesser view of the Bible than that of our Master?

Before one can evaluate any system of teaching, he should carefully research the claims and nature of the Bible. "The word of God, . . . liveth and abideth forever" (I Peter 1:23). (See also Psalm 138:2; II Peter 1:18-21.)

Chapter 8

Pseudo-Christian Cults

"But there were false prophets also among the people, even as there shall be false teachers among you, who privily shall bring in damnable heresies, even denying the Lord that bought them, and bring upon themselves swift destruction. And many shall follow their pernicious ways; by reason of whom the way of truth shall be evil spoken of" (II Peter 2:1-2).

This strong statement is an apt preface to this chapter in which we will discuss both false "Christian" cults and bad fellowships. Some of these sects look very much like real Christianity. At the conclusion of this chapter we will give some marks of identification by which one can spot such a cult.

The Worldwide Church of God

On July 24, 1976, Herbert W. Armstrong boldly stated:

"The gospel has not been preached until God raised me up to preach it. People say, 'Who does that Armstrong think he is?' Am I bragging? Am I boasting? No, I am just saying a fact. That gospel you never heard from any preacher except one from this church. You never heard it from Billy Graham. You never heard it from any Protestant preacher. You never heard it from any Catholic priest" (*Ambassador Report,* p. 13).

Yet, the Bible says that "no prophecy of the Scripture is of any private interpretation" (II Peter 1:20).

Armstrong founded the Worldwide Church of God in 1934 with a radio program and a paper, *The Plain Truth.* Today, of all the cults, the WCG sponsors more radio and television programs than any other. The promotional techniques of the WCG have been very successful. The publications are slick and deal with sensational themes, spectacular predictions, and exclusivistic claims. The image of unwavering faithfulness to the Word of God is strongly projected, in this day when many old-line churches are denying the Word. The WCG magazines decry the breakdown of the family, the moral decay of society, and the increase of crime. Supposedly only the WCG has the answer to the problems and hope for the future. Only they are dispensers of God's truth.

How Plain Is the Truth?

Armstrongism is a denial of the Godhead (the doctrine of the Trinity). This is a common error among the cults and you should familiarize yourself with the Scripture passages on the Trinity. (For example: Genesis 1:26; Isaiah 48:16; Matthew 3:16-17, 28:19; Romans 1:20; Colossians 2:9.)

The WCG denies the deity of Jesus. According to Armstrong, a person cannot be saved here and now. There is no continued existence of the soul. Only believers will be resurrected. Armstrong has made many dated predictions of "the end," all of which have failed. This cult seems to be a strange mixture of Mormonism, Jehovah's Witness, and British Israelism.

The Worldwide Church of God has recently been split by Garner Ted Armstrong, son of the founder, who leads the new body. In spite of this, and other troubles, there is every indication that the cult will continue to grow.

Jim Jones and the People's Temple

The Jonestown suicide-massacre will go down in history as one of the darkest events in modern times. On November 19, 1978, guns blazed as the followers of Jim Jones opened fire on Congressman Leo Ryan and his party at the Port Kaituma, Guyana, airfield. Jones then urged his followers in the colony, 8 miles away, to commit suicide. The next day, over 900 bodies lay dead beneath the tropic sun. Out of what dark abyss of hell does a tragedy of this magnitude proceed?

Many thought the People's Temple in San Francisco was another sect of Christianity. Jones had, at various times, been a minister in the Unitarian, Methodist, Pentecostal, and

Disciples of Christ churches. But Jones scoffed at the Bible, cursed it, and is a prime example of apostasy. He demanded that his followers engage in illicit sexual acts. Beatings were common. He "faked" healings. His love for Communism is now well known. Early in his career, Jones was deeply impressed by a visit to Father Divine in Philadelphia. Later, Jones claimed to be god. His mind control over his subjects was illustrated by the obedience shown in Guyana when suicide was demanded.

Children of God

Memorization of long Bible passages is a specialty of the Children of God (COG). This makes a strong impression on youth with a fundamental Bible background. The cult distorts Scripture and promotes hatred of family, the establishment, and the church.

The COG movement began under the leadership of David Berg, who now goes by the name of Moses David. In 1971, three prominent members of the Jesus People movement defected to the COG and things started rolling. There are now over 120 communes with a few thousand members in 65 countries. Errors of the COG include immorality, Biblical distortion, occultism, and allegiance to a man rather than God. Followers believe Moses David is God's prophet for the last days and he is to be followed blindly.

Moses David grinds out "MO Letters" on a variety of sensational and weird subjects. These letters are used for street distribution, called "litnessing," and indoctrination of followers. Several of the letters teach spiritism (communication with the dead — see chapter 11). Moses David prophesied the destruction of the United States would occur on January 31, 1974 — another date-setting scheme that fizzled. The movement is constantly cited for immorality, and one can read in a MO Letter:

"We have a sexy God with a sexy religion and a very sexy leader and an extremely sexy young following. . . . Salvation sets us free from the curse of clothing and the shame of nakedness."

Young women of the COG are pressured to use sex to lure men (especially the wealthy) into the cult, or to support the cult. Former members testify that men were urged to prostitute their wives for the "sake of the kingdom." (Note I Timothy 2:9.)

The COG has recently made a fresh start using the name "Family of Love." Watch out for them. At first glance they seem to be orthodox in doctrine, zealous in witnessing, and Pentecostal in worship. Once on the inside, however, one discovers corruption, spiritism, and a host of false doctrines. They seem superspiritual and have trapped a number of our youth.

The Way

One of the cleverest deceptions is "The Way," led by Victor Paul Wierwille. One is given the impression that this group is orthodox, evangelical, and Pentecostal (members are "taught" to speak in tongues). In the meetings one can hear expressions similar to those heard in evangelical churches, such as: "the Lord Jesus Christ," "the Holy Spirit," the "Son of God," and "the blood of Jesus." However, Wierwille says: "Many people may be misled because while using the same language or words we don't mean the same thing" (*Jesus Christ is Not God* [New Knoxville, OH: American Christian Press, The Way International, 1975] p. 4). The Way teaches that Jesus is only eternal in that He was in the foreknowledge of God. He is a created being. However, in Isaiah 9:6 the coming Messiah is described as a human child who is also "the mighty God." Wierwille's teaching that Jesus only came into being at the Incarnation contradicts Micah 5:2. (Also compare John 17:5 with Isaiah 42:8.)

Victor Paul Wierwille, founder of "The Way," is a graduate of Moody Bible Institute and Princeton Seminary. The movement began in 1953 when Wierwille held his first "Power for Abundant Living Class." It did not experience much growth until 1968 when two men from the Jesus Movement joined forces with The Way. Conservative estimates say there are now about 20,000 adherents. By taking courses at $85 and up entrance is made into the group. *Christianity Today* asserts that The Way is gaining about 1,000 new members monthly.

The Way is sending missionaries all over the world. They have a college with over 400 students in Emporia, Kansas.

The organization is structured as "The Way Tree," with the "trunk" being the international headquarters; "limbs" are state offices; "twigs," local home or campus meetings; and individual members, "leaves."

The Way of Victor Paul Wierwille is not the way of Jesus Christ, and it will not lead one to the Father or to eternal life. It is true, however, that there are Christians in the ranks because enlistment has been heavy among evangelical Christians — not because The Way is winning souls.

The True Way

Jesus is the true way (John 14:6). He is God. Anyone who denies this agrees with antichrist rather then the Bible (I John 2:18-23, especially v. 22). The Church has always agreed on the foundational concept of the deity of Jesus, as stated by the confession of the council of Nicea (AD 325).:

"We believe . . . in one Lord Jesus Christ, the son of God, . . . [of the substance of the Father] God of God, . . . [very God of very God, begotten, not made, of one substance with the Father], through whom all was made, . . . came down and became flesh. But those who say there was when He was not, and before being begotten He was not, and was made out of things that were not, or those who say that the Son of God was from a different substance or being, or a creature, or capable of change or alteration, these the church anathematizes (curses)."

The Local Church

The Local Church was started in Los Angeles in 1962 by a Chinese man who calls himself Witness Lee. He is sometimes confused with Watchman Nee, a highly respected Christian leader and author in China. Lee was, at one time, a disciple of Nee. The most notable trait of the Local Church is exclusiveness. Lee holds that his group is the only church approved by God. He writes in *The Practical Expression of the Church*:

"We need to have our eyes opened, for if we have not seen the Local Church we are in darkness and under a blindfold . . . The only way to follow the Lord absolutely is to go the way of the Local Church" (pages 31, 32, 94).

It takes an extreme arrogance to declare that all Christians of all time were in darkness because they did not belong to his movement.

The true church of Christ includes all born-again believers regardless of denominational affiliation (I Corinthians 12:27). The term *church* can apply to all the believers in a given city or locality, as in "the church of God which is at Corinth" (I Corinthians 1:2).

When Witness Lee's followers chant their oft-repeated slogan, "One city, one church," they are not saying that all members of the Local Church must meet in one place; their goal for Los Angeles is 100 meeting places. What they really are saying is that everyone must join Lee's exclusive group or be lost.

Their pray-reading, chanting worship is like Eastern and Hindu chanting, and the members seem brainwashed. Lee wrote: "There is no need for us to close our eyes when we pray. It is better to close your mind" (*Pray Reading*, pp. 8-10). Lee discourages studying the Bible, even though Paul wrote: "Study to show thyself approved . . ." (II Timothy 2:15). (See also I Timothy 4:16).

John Todd and the Illuminati

A strange influence has been wielded by a young man who claims to have been a member of the Illuminati, headed by Philip Rothschild of London (a nonexistent person). He claims "insider" knowledge of the world conspiracy for world government headed by the super rich and the occult.

John Todd was "converted" at Castle Hills Baptist Church in San Antonio on Labor Day, 1972. Although he says he never considered Jesus before 1972, we have discovered he had a conversion experience in a charismatic church in Columbus, Ohio, in 1966, and was in a Jesus Only Church in Phoenix in 1968.

Todd accuses Jimmy Carter of being the Antichrist, the coming world ruler. He claims that while he was on the "grand druid council" he delivered millions of dollars to various corrupt leaders of the charismatic movement; he names names. On a tape distributed by a prominent prophecy teacher, Todd accuses the Assemblies of God of being taken over by the Illuminati conspiracy.

Since he claims secret information as a former "insider," there seems to some to be authority in what he says. However, we have carefully researched Todd and his claims, listened to about 70 hours of his taped lectures, and interviewed many who have known him for years, and we can report positively that Todd has fantasized his role in the Illuminati. He was never a member of such a world conspiracy as he describes. He did not even meet the charismatic leaders he accuses until after his alleged conversion from the Illuminati in 1972.

Although Todd says that speaking in tongues is witchcraft, he still gets a following among Pentecostals and charismatics, as well as in fundamentalist circles. He holds no hope for end-time revival, stating that the only revival there will be will be a revival of witchcraft and satanism. Todd's problem is that his devil is bigger than his God. He encourages Christians to sell their homes, prepare a retreat, and buy food supplies for survival and guns for defense. This is in spite of the fact that he preaches a pre-Tribulation Rapture.

Todd taught that there would be riots and revolution in the fall of 1979. President Carter would declare martial law and there would never again be a free election of a U.S. president. Carter would become a dictator and, through the Tri-Lateral Commission, the ruler of the European block of nations.

John Todd may be saying some things that are true, but his teaching is so mixed with error, wild accusations, and false predictions that he should not be heeded by anyone. His long history of immoral conduct, several marriages (both common law and legal), and his lapses into witchcraft since "conversion," do not recommend him as a spokesman for God in the last days. John Todd has been a powerfully divisive force in segments of the evangelical realm, worldwide. (See Romans 16:17.)

The Bible Speaks
Carl Stevens, a former Baptist minister, launched The Bible Speaks in 1962. Its headquarters is located in Lenox, Massachusetts. This cult is extremely subtle, and there are many others similar to it. Some unwary Christians have joined The Bible Speaks, thinking it to be a fundamental, Bible-teaching church. Indeed, you could not fault most points

of their statement of faith. This statement projects the image of a Pentecostal or charismatic church with its emphasis on the work of the Holy Spirit and the gifts of the Spirit. There is great emphasis on the supernatural.

Stevens claims to have had a vision from God in which He told him that every sermon he preached would be directly from God, with full divine authority. Even the Pope only claims infallibility on occasions! Stevens seems to have it all the time! Since his pronouncements come directly from heaven, Stevens demands absolute obedience not only in spiritual matters but also in every realm. He has demanded that wives leave their husbands and then remarry a spouse of his choosing. He demands obedience in money matters. He declares that anyone who speaks against him or The Bible Speaks is rebelling against God and will be severely punished.

There is an almost worshipful attitude displayed toward Stevens. He is thought to be infallible and his gift of prophecy equal to the Bible. In his *Book of Miracles* (published by The Bible Speaks), there is a section "about the pastor" (Stevens) which says:

"What was it like to walk with Jesus, to see His smile, to be looked upon with that piercing glance? . . . What was it like to laugh with Him, to cry with Him . . . to be His friend? Most Christians have wondered at this one time or another. Those in The Bible Speaks stopped wondering years ago. To be a sheep under the shepherdship of Pastor Carl Stevens is to know intimately the person of the Lord."

It is all right to lie under certain circumstances if you are a member of The Bible Speaks. The *Phoenix* (a Boston newspaper) reported:

"Mrs. Dunham believes her daughter and sister lie to the family and outsiders in general about what is going on inside The Bible Speaks. 'They believe it's all right to lie to protect Carl Stevens and the Group.' . . . The Weymouth Children also said they had been told at school that anyone not of The Bible Speaks is of Satan and that it is all right to deceive Satan."

This is loaded with false assumptions.

The *Phoenix* also cites cases of students being severely beaten by staff members of The Bible Speaks. In one case, teenagers were beaten with a stick "to drive the devil" out of them. The dorm father administering the punishment kept saying, "The Lord told me to do this to you." In talking of this case, Cumberland County District Attorney said: "He beat . . . them with a wooden chair leg. . . . The Kids' buttocks looked like hamburger in the colored photographs." The judge meted out a 6-month suspended sentence to the dorm father. The parents of the teenagers instituted a lawsuit for $110,500 against The Bible Speaks. The *Phoenix* stated that the dorm father was still with The Bible Speaks in Lenox.

Bad Fellowships

This chapter contains only a few examples of pseudo-Christian cults. Some of these groups are hard to classify since there seems to be acceptance of the Word of God in certain cases, but they cannot be accepted because of bad practices or conduct.

In dealing with borderline cases, standard doctrinal tests for heresy or cultism may not apply. Therefore, we must look at behavioral rather than doctrinal patterns. There are a number of warning signals to watch for, such as organizational bondage, psychological dependence or mind control, and financial exploitation. Watch out for groups that have one-man leadership. Be wary of those whose major thrust is the penetration of existing evangelical groups to win converts, rather than reaching the lost with the gospel. Pray for the gift of "discerning of spirits" (I Corinthians 12:10).

Chapter 9

The Unification Church

Sun Myung Moon was born on January 8, 1920 in North Korea, the second of eight children of a farmer. During his boyhood his family joined the Korean Presbyterian Church. Moon later attended high school in Seoul. There he also attended a Pentecostal church.

Another Gospel Is Born

At 15, Moon received a "revelation," and came to realize that unless he saved the world, it was doomed to continue to be burdened with sin and suffering. So Moon took on himself the burden of liberating the entire human race. Speaking about his youth, Moon says:

"From childhood, I was clairvoyant and clairaudient. . . . When I was 12 years old, I started praying for extraordinary things. I asked for wisdom greater than Solomon's, for faith greater than Apostle Paul's, and for love greater than the love Jesus had. . . . When I was 16 I knew definitely what my mission was to be" ("The Master Speaks on the Lord of the Second Advent," *MS-1*, March-April 1965, p. 1).

Moon was speaking of the first of many such experiences. This vision was to be the spiritual foundation for Moon's church, The Holy Spirit Association for the Unification of World Christianity.

According to Moon, Jesus appeared to him on Easter morning, 1936, to tell him he had been selected to finish the work Jesus had failed to complete. This spirit asked Moon to restore

God's perfect kingdom — to become the completer of man's salvation by becoming the second coming of Christ.

Moon was reluctant to accept this "divine" assignment, knowing that once he did there would be no turning back. But Jesus pleaded that Moon "was the only one who could do it, and asked him again and again." Finally, Moon accepted the task, knowing no other person could ever replace him should he fail. Since the spirit that appeared to Moon preached a gospel drastically different from the Bible, there can be no question that spirit was a demon (Galatians 1:8).

Unification Church Comes Into Being

During World War II, Moon studied electrical engineering in Tokyo, while continuing to receive new revelations from spirits. In *The Divine Principle* we read that "he fought alone against myriads of satanic forces, both in the spiritual and physical worlds, and finally triumphed over them all" (The Holy Spirit Association for the Unification of World Christianity, 1973, p. 16).

After 1945, he began making his new revelations known, and was soon excommunicated by the Korean Presbyterian Church. He then established a church of his own and continued preaching. According to a U.S. Government publication, the Moon movement was far less influential in Korea than elsewhere. In fact, most Koreans had not heard of Moon until his activities began to be publicized in the 1970's.

Time of Persecution

After World War II, Moon was in and out of Korean prisons. Moon states that he was jailed three times, but Unification propaganda usually implies he was imprisoned once. In his speeches, Moon frequently speaks of those days:

"The police came and an innocent man received a terrible beating; pints of blood flowed from an internal injury. He lost consciousness. His broken body was thrown outside" (Jerry Yamamoto, *The Puppet Master* [Downers Grove, IL: Inter-Varsity Press, 1977]).

Moon's sufferings were to play an important role in his developing ideology. *The Divine Principle* claims: "He endured suffering unimagined by anyone in human history"

Moon states: "I had to go through severe hardships culminating in the torture of prison life, which was more for me than Jesus' cross" (*Master Speaks* [Speeches by Moon.] May 27, 1973). When Moon suffered he "payed indemnity." This is the primary doctrine of the Unification Church, which insists that we must do likewise. Moon states: "I have paid a great amount of indemnity, and because of this I have the right to forgive another's sins" (The Master Speaks on Prayer and the Spirit World," *MS-3*, p. 16). There was another benefit to Moon's sufferings:

"I always had to thank God, because only by putting me under hardship could he cultivate and train me to be the *leader of the world*" (*Investigation of Korean-American Relations*, Government Printing Office, October 31, 1978, p. 1217). [Italics mine.]

Moonrise Over America

Moon then began his American campaigns, arriving in Los Angeles with the announcement: "I did not come for the luxurious life in America" (*The Puppet Master*). On his first tour, he called on Americans to abandon their denominational affiliations for a real relationship with God through the second coming of Chirst.

During his second tour, the media became fascinated with Moon because of his near-fanatical support of Nixon during the Watergate crisis. In fact, at the end of the tour, Nixon personally thanked Moon in the White House for his support. It was a much-photographed media event, and probably had quite a bit to do with Moon's mushrooming ego. In a speech that he gave soon afterward, Moon purred: "Everybody knows that . . . Reverend Moon has saved Nixon and America" (*Investigation of Korean-American Relations*, p. 1148).

But, during Moon's third speaking tour, Christian groups greeted him with organized protests and vigorous demonstrations. Nevertheless, Moon was granted "permanent resident alien" immigration status by the Department of Labor in 1973. He currently resides in a $620,000 estate in Tarrytown, New York, and can frequently be found cruising in one of his two $250,000 yachts. His personal wealth is reported to be $15 million, much to the delight of his followers, who live extremely spartan lives. Addressing future Unification Church leaders, senior Moonie, Ken Sudo, states:

"Do you like to make green bills happy? . . . They are all destined to go to Father [Moon]. This is our responsibility. . . . Christians think that the Messiah must be poor and miserable. He did not come for this. Messiah must be the richest." (120-Day Training Manual, p. 72).

Unification Church Beliefs

Like many other cults, the Unification Church has a maze of secret beliefs. These are described in secret Unification Church documents, such as the 120-Day Training Manual and Master Speaks, copies of which have been made available by defecting Moonies. When questioned about his inner beliefs, the typical Moonie will attempt to sidestep the question or will openly lie, having been taught that "heavenly deception" is approved by God.

Can Moon Be the Son?

One of the most important beliefs centers on Moon himself. Just who is he? The secret 120-Day Training Manual tells us:

"Then they can understand that Rev. Moon is Messiah, Lord of the Second Advent" (p. 160).

"Christians will be guided to the Lord of the Second Advent, and can understand that he is the Messiah. Then Christians will bow to him and say my Lord has come again" (p. 226).

"Father [Moon] is visible God" (p. 362).

"Father's body is [the] temple of God" (p. 116).

"Father is sinless, Mother [Moon's latest wife] is sinless, and their children are sinless. . . . If we can't have any relationship with the Messiah's family, we have nothing to do with salvation" (p. 236).

"He [Moon] . . . can solve my sin and he can be my savior" (p. 222).

Moon has more than a few words to describe himself. Speaking about himself in the third person, Moon states: "Our Leader, being a perfect Son of god, came down to your level. He doesn't need prayer" ("The Master Speaks on the Restoration and Judgement," MS-4(2), p. 10). Another time,

Moon stated: "After hearing me, public opinion about Rev. Moon changed. They could see that he is the hero of the world" (*Investigation of Korean-American Relations*, p. 1215).

Moon believes that he knows more than Jesus:

"I have talked with many masters, including Jesus. . . . They have subjected themselves to me in terms of wisdom. After winning the victory, they surrendered" ("The Master Speaks on Prayer and the Spirit World," *MS 3*, p. 4).

Being smarter than Jesus, Moon feels qualified to do all of the thinking for his people. Moon says: "I am a thinker. I am your brain" (*Investigation of Korean-American Relations*, p. 1058).

More About the Divine Principle

The Divine Principle states:

"It may be displeasing to religious believers, especially to Christians, to learn that a new expression of truth must appear. They believe that the Bible, which they now have, is perfect and absolute. . . . The Bible, however, is not the truth itself, but a textbook teaching the truth. . . . We must not regard the testbook as absolute in every detail" (p. 9).

Although Moon himself did not write *The Divine Principle*, he was the one who wrested its secrets from the spirit world. The secret *120-Day Training Manual* states:

"After severe trial, Father's truth was approved by Jesus and by God. The contents of his research and his victory was declared as Divine Principle. This is why Divine Principle can be called the truth. . . . The truth through which man can obtain perfection" (p. 114).

Moon says: "The [Divine] Principle is not the word of man, but the Word of God" ("The Master Speaks on Prayer and the Spirit World," *MS-3*, p. 8).

In an attempt to diminish its authority, *The Divine Principle* claims that the Bible will lose its light. *The Divine Principle* denies both the deity and the bodily resurrection of Christ, and claims that He failed to complete His earthly mission. It opens the door for Moon's pseudo-secret claims to be the Messiah, by claiming that the Messiah's second coming will be realized when he is born on earth. In one of the few places where *The Divine Principle* agrees with the Bible, it states that all men are sinners. Unfortunately, it doesn't explain who forgave Rev. Sun Myung Moon's sins. (See *The Divine Principle*, pp. 118, 209-212, 141-143, 502, 2.)

Moon's Jesus, Made in Korea

Moon is a man of many words, and almost never uses one word when 20 will do. But, somehow, he always gets right to the point when denying Christ. For example:

"Jesus lost everything on the cross . . . Jesus failed his mission by dying on the cross. . . . You must make it clear that the Lord of the Second Advent is coming in the place of Jesus" (*Investigation of Korean-American Relations*, pp. 1029, 1214, 1215).

The *120-Day Training Manual* says: "We must love others instead of Jesus" (p. 165).

Moon and the Christian Church

If Moon is nothing else, he is consistent. Just as he claims to replace Jesus, so the Unification Church replaces the Christian Church. As Moon puts it:

"Christianity is failing its task, so our group must take it up. . . . It is an amazing thing. Through the Divine Principle, all areas of thought, even Christianity, . . . can easily be understood" (*Investigation of Korean-American Relations*, pp. 1123, 1131).

But all does not set well in Moon's attitude toward the true church of Jesus Christ.

"We know those who hate the Unification Church most are Christian people. Those Christians don't want to hate us; they hate us because Satan is in them. . . . Now when they are against us, then they are going to get the punishment. . . . Every people or every organization that goes against the Unification Church will gradually come down or drastically come down and die. Many people will die — those who go against our movement" (*Investigation of Korean-American Relations*, pp. 1080, 1089).

These are very strange words from the same man who said: "I am truly the most noble and precious VIP that ever came to America. . . . I am a prophet, a messenger of God" (Investigation of Korean-American Relations, *p. 1243*).

The Unification Church and the Occult

The secret documents reveal startling facts about the Unification Church practices. But first let us review God's Word about dealing with the occult. Leviticus 19:31 and 20:27 give God's clear warning to have nothing to do with those who contact "familiar spirits." A familiar spirit is a demon. Modern Bible translations indicate that people who talk with familiar spirits are called "mediums."

The Amplified Bible states: "A man or a woman who is a medium and has a familiar spirit or is a wizard, shall surely be put to death" (Leviticus 20:27). But Moon doesn't see it this way. His instructions for dealing with new converts are:

"Teach the [Divine] Principle first, intellectually, and guide the student to the spiritual experience by having him read books on the spirit world or by taking him to a medium" ("The Master Speaks on the Second Advent," *MS-1*, p. 5).

Moon instructs: "Yes it is good to have one or two mediumistic people in the group who will help others to grow spiritually" ("The Master Speaks on Prayer and the Spirit World," MS-3, p. 5).

The demons that Moon's mediums contact are quite real. One Moonie said: "I don't feel worthy to talk to God yet, but I feel perfectly free to talk with the spirits who are working with me" ("The Master Speaks on Prayer and the Spirit World," p. 15). But Moon cautions:

"Most spirits are very selfish. They want to control you and use you. It is always dangerous . . . to be controlled by [a] spirit. But by understanding the Principle, . . . you can control and use and guide them" (The Master Speaks on Prayer and the Spirit World," p. 16).

According to Moon, if his people understand the Divine Principle, they can control and use the same "spirits" who are seeking to control and use them. But this is far from true, according to the *120-Day Training Manual:*

"This is the reason why when a Divine Principle lecture is going on or after a Divine Principle lecture someone may become possessed" (p. 144).

The *120-Day Training Manual*, describes a number of cases of demon possession among Moonies:

"When an evil spirit can utilize the physical body of another person, he doesn't care at all if this physical body is broken or not. He drives the physical body as he likes. The character changes at once. The physical body is the same, but he is a completely different person. . . ."

"Before I came to Barrytown . . . one brother got possessed . . . Maybe even five brothers cannot catch a possessed person because he becomes very strong, and this means so much exhaustion of the physical body. Possession is terrible on the physical body. . . ."

"I know of another case in Japan where someone because of spiritual possession died. And it became big trouble. . . . This spiritual problem is not so easy" (pp. 143, 144).

What do the Moonies do when one of them becomes possessed? There are instructions in the secret documents, but the instructions themselves declare that they usually don't work. The final solution is tragic:

"In case it is impossible to stop the possession . . . send the person to a hospital. Also, let the person's physical parents know what is going on" (*120-Day Training Manual,* pp. 145, 146).

In spite of these horror stories, Moon continues to advise his followers to deal with mediums and their demons.

Summary

Moon's new cult is merely the old occult with Korean window dressing. The secret documents reveal that Moon offers a more direct path to hell than most other cults. *The Divine Principle* contains a collection of "new revelations" that contradict the Word of God.

The Bible does not view Jesus' sacrifice as unintended by God or as incomplete. Isaiah 53 reveals Jesus as our one true Messiah (John 4:25-26). Peter states that the Lord's sacrifice was God's plan, foreknown by Him (Acts 2:23), and describes the utter foolishness of looking to anyone else for salvation (Acts 4:12). Moon's claim to have provided for mankind's physical salvation (which he says Jesus failed to do) is preposterous.

Christians now await the redemption of their bodies (Romans 8:23), which is guaranteed as part of the rapture of the Church (I Corinthians 15:50-55). It is equally preposterous to call the Christian Church a failure, in the light of Matthew 16:18. Moon's denial of the literal appearing of Christ in the clouds contradicts Matthew 24:30, 26:64; Luke 21:27; Titus 2:13; Revelation 19:13-16, 22:20. The Word leaves no room for any other "messiah" (Matthew 24:23-27).

The Unification Church's use of mediums is an abomination before God (Deuteronomy 18:10-12), and the sad results of Sun Myung Moon's occultism are a frightful thing. Moon brings no deliverance to the world. Our answer to Moon's claims is clear! We will follow Jesus Christ.

Chapter 10

Eastern Religions

The coming world religion of the Antichrist and the false prophet will be both humanistic and satanic. It will be humanistic in that the beast will demand and receive worship (II Thessalonians 2:3-4; Revelation 13:8). It is hard to imagine a political leader being worshiped universally as god, but the devil is very clever.

Satan will, no doubt, have his puppet (Revelation 13:4) Antichrist say: "We have abolished all religions and sects except for the new world religion of humanism. When you bow to worship me you are worshiping the deity of all humanity. Only man is divine. There is no other god."

The beast and false prophet demonstrate great satanic powers and will work miracles. Paul writes of the man of sin "whose coming is after the working of Satan with all power and signs and lying wonders" (II Thessalonians 2:9). The false prophet "deceiveth them that dwell on the earth by the means of those miracles which he had power to do in the sight of the beast" (Revelation 13:14).

Decades ago it would have been hard to envision our Western civilization being carried away with Satan's slick sideshow of supernaturalism. But with the advance of Eastern mysticism, it is no longer hard to see how this will come about. There is a strange likeness between humanism (see chapter 5) and the Eastern philosophies. Humanism declares there is no god but man. The Eastern mystics speak of many "god" concepts, but finally their "god" is to be found within man's own nature. Their mantras and meditations are to help us find god within ourselves.

Professor W.A. McKeever (formerly of the University of Kansas) could be speaking for either camp:

"I worship God through man. To know God is first to know man and to know man is to worship the divinity in him. . . . Man is my best expression of deity, and so I bow reverently at this shrine" (W.A. McKeever, *Man and the New Democracy*).

End-Time Spiritual Warfare

As we approach the end of the age the battle intensifies. Satan is deternimed to penetrate and take over Christian civilization. I see his messengers on the streets and whenever I go through an airport. Theologian Nels Ferre may have been stating the case too strongly for some when he wrote in 1961:

"The main fight, make no mistake, is between the Christian faith in its inner classical meaning and the new Orientalized versions, whether they come via neo-Platonism or in modern forms. . . . The supernatural, personalistic, classical Christian faith is now being undermined by an ultimately nondualistic, impersonal or transpersonal faith. The winds are blowing gale-strong out of the Orient" (Surjit Singh, *Christianity and Personality*, foreward; as cited by Brooks Alexander, *Occult Philosophy*, Spiritual Counterfeits Project pamphlet).

Today no one would look at Ferre's words as an overstatement.

In this end-time struggle for souls we must never lose sight of the fact that there is but one way to the Father, and that is through Jesus. That is why the Saviour spoke of a narrow way to life and a broad way that leads to destruction.

Mystery Babylon

The harlot of Revelation 17 and 18 may be speaking of the end-time religious occult system that "rides on the back of the beast" (political system under the Antichrist). She is noted for her sorceries (Revelation 18:23). Ultimately, the beast destroys her. The Antichrist uses the blended world religion composed of apostate Christendom and other world religions, but finally sweeps all that is worshiped aside, so he alone can sit in the temple of God (II Thessalonians 2:4).

As the true Church is the bride of Christ, the harlot religion is the mistress of the beast. Whereas Jesus loves His Church and conforts her, the beast hates his mistress and destroys her. In his far-reaching prophecy against Babylon, Isaiah recognized the harlot and pronounced her doom. (Isaiah 47:1-5, 13-15). The prophet Nahum met her at Nineveh:

"Because of the multitude of the whoredoms of the well-favored harlot, the mistress of witchcrafts, that selleth nations through her whoredoms, and families through her witchcrafts. Behold, I am against thee, saith the Lord of hosts" (Nahum 3:4-5). (Compare this passage and Isaiah 47 with Revelation 17 and 18.)

What is said here about the Eastern cults can be said, in some degree, about all cults. They are all the devil's troops in his last-ditch stand against the church of Jesus Christ as the climax of the age approaches. But, thank God, the gates of hell shall not prevail against the Church (Matthew 16:18-19). Now that we have this overview of the subject, let us look at some specific cults.

International Society for Krishna Consciousness

Members of the Hare Krishna cult allegedly worship "one god," Krishna. However, in their book *Srimad Bhagavatam* it says:

"One should worship Lord Vishu or His devotee for spiritual advancement in knowledge, and for protection of heredity and advancement of a dynasty one should worship the various demigods" (Los Angeles: Bhaktivedanta Book Trust, 1977, p. 141).

Krishna worship is an ancient Indian Hindu cult. It has been chiefly imported to the United States by "His Divine Grace" Abhay Charan De Bhaktivedanta Swami Prabhupada. He was, in early life, a follower of the Hindu holy man, Bhaktisiddhanta Saraswati, who initiated him into the Goudiya Vaishnava Society. In 1936, his master ordered him to bring the message to the English-speaking world. So in 1954, at the age of 58, Prabhupada abandoned his wife and five children to obey his master's command. He donned the saffron yellow robes of a hindu monk and became a "swami."

In 1965, almost 30 years after his "call," he arrived in the United States. Under a tree in Tompkins Park, he sat and chanted the names of Krishna. During the following year his first temple was established in New York. And 1968 marked the beginning of ISKCON'S magazine, *Back to Godhead*. Today, devotees can be seen everywhere selling books and incense, and begging for money. You might see a group of them in their yellow robes in a park or sitting on a street, chanting, "Hare Krishna, Hare, Hare, Hare, Rama."

ISKCON has built a lavish center, open to the public, near Moundsville, West Virginia. Rather than contempt, we must show these deluded people the love of Jesus as we share our witness. Satan would like us to either write them off as "nuts" or accept them as brothers without their knowing the saving grace of Calvary. We must avoid both extremes when dealing with cultists.

Guru Ma

One of the most colorful gurus (spiritual leaders) on the scene today is Elizabeth Clare Prophet, widow of Mark Prophet, the founder of Summit Lighthouse, now known as the Church Universal and Triumphant. This fairly new cult, founded in 1958, received its direction originally from teachings of "Master El Morya Khan of India," who called himself "God of Divine Will." Elizabeth was Mark's convert prior to their marriage. The Prophets declared themselves to be the messengers of "The Great White Brotherhood of Ascended Masters." The brotherhood includes such greats as Confucius, Buddha, Saint Francis, Mary the mother of Jesus, and Jesus himself. Thus, they reduced Jesus to the status of being just "one of the boys."

These "masters" communicate through spiritistic methods, and the cult is nothing more than spiritualism. Mrs. Prophet clearly stated: "I am that I am [the name of God in Exodus 3:14] is really your own Godself"; and, "The only real moral choice we have to make in our lives is 'to be or not to be God.'" Guru Ma, as she bills herself, is making a lot of appearances on college campuses and seems to be gaining a large following.

Yoga

Yoga is another Far Eastern philosophy that is particularly deceptive and subtle, in that many think they can practice yoga exercises (hatha yoga) without embracing the spiritual aspect. I do not believe this is possible. The word *yoga* means mystical union (with the Universal Spirit). Some frank teachers of yoga have clearly revealed that the purpose of physical yoga is to lead to spiritual yoga. One teacher says:

"The sole purpose of the physical practices of Hatha Yoga is to suppress physical obstacles on the Spiritual or Royal path of Raja Yoga; and Hatha Yoga is therefore called the ladder to Raja Yoga" (Alain Danielou, *Yoga: The Method of Re-Integration* [New York: University Books, 1955], p. 17).

The goal of yoga is self-realization (finding god within). One must aim at attaining his eternal self through the practice of many exercises in purification. Some doctors recommend the practice of Hatha Yoga for health reasons. Classes are taught in churches and the YWCA. Those who think they can do the physical yoga exercises and go no further are skating on thin ice. In some classes, the teacher may have students repeat short phrases in an Indian language during the exercises. They are not told that these are Hindu or Buddhist prayers. Christians who have tried yoga report a loss of spiritual power and awareness of Jesus, and a decreasing desire to read the Bible.

Eckankar

If you have even heard of *Eckankar,* you may think it is a very small, minor cult. But actually, it has an estimated membership in the United States of 50,000 (compared with Moon's hard-core U.S. membership of only about 10,000). Paul Twitchell built this cult into a multimillion-dollar business specializing in selling literature, Akashic and Eck-Vidya readings ($60 to $150), jewelry, and cassette tapes. Twitchell started the movement in 1964, and claims mystical Eastern influence as its inspiration. In 1955, he was initiated into "Ruhani Satsang" by yogi Kirpal Singh. In 1958 he was associated with Ron Hubbard's Scientology (see chapter 5).

What is Eckankar? Here are Twitchell's own words:

"My saints are Kabir, 16th-century Hindu mystical poet

who taught Sabda Marg, the path of Shabda Yoga. Other saints I follow are the ancient Sufi avatars Jalal al-din Rumi, Hafi, Shamus-i-Tabiz, Rama, the Indian Savior, and Kirpal Singh of India. Eckankar, which I formed out of my own experience, is the term used for the philosophy I have developed for the Cliff Hanger. It is based on Shabda Yoga.''

In addition to the readings (made for individuals seeking guidance and fulfillment), a major teaching is astral projection or soul travel. I have, in my possession, an original hand-written letter from Twitchell to one of his followers, in which he says: "Your former wife was in the life of King Solomon — see reading. Your children were with you in Atlantis.''

The recipient of the letter rejected Eckankar and many other forms of occultism when he accepted Christ as Saviour. How could he do otherwise, knowing how Twitchell hated Christ?

"The whole pack of them will start spouting something they have read in the scriptures. . . . They quote Jesus as their authority and scream about His love for each of them personally. None of which is true" (Twitchell, *The Tiger's Fang* [Las Vegas: Eckankar, 1967], p. 170).

Twitchell died in 1971. Since then Sri Darwin Gross has been the leader of the movement.

A Multitude of Mystics

There are so many Eastern mystics it would be impossible to even list, let alone define, them all in this chapter. Here are a few short comments on several:

Bubba Free John. "I am Reality, the Self, and Nature and Support of all things and all beings. I am the One Being, known as God, Brahman, Altman, the One Mind, the Self.'' This cult has Hindu roots. His following was enlarged by college campus appearances.

Maharaj Ji: He is a young Hindu guru, popular among American youth and entertainers. His organization is called the Divine Light Mission. He claims to be the Second Coming of Christ, "the one and only perfect master for this age.''

Rosicrucianism: The followers claim the movement started in ancient Egypt. They advertise widely in popular magazines. There are about 250,000 in the United States. They teach: God is impersonal, reincarnation, and man is evolving into a divine being.

I Ching: This is not an organized cult, but a book. It is a Chinese means of divination for guidance. It involves tossing sticks and coins. Journalist, Peter Rowley, claims it has "up to 600,000 followers in America."

Zen Buddhism: Buddhism began as a reformation within Hinduism. Zen is difficult to define. Zen Buddhists try to go beyond reason through meditating on irrational problems to gain a flash of insight or enlightenment beyond reason. Salvation is achieved through self.

Holy Order of Mans: This group claims to be Christian, but teaches the occult/Eastern view that Jesus was a great teacher, but a mere man. The leaders preach realization of the god-self. It was founded in San Francisco in 1968 by Earl Blighton. This cult now has three seminaries, 100 missionary centers, and hundreds of male and female priests, who wear garb like Roman Catholic clergy.

Baha'i

In concluding this chapter we will deal with the Baha'i faith which denies the sinful nature of man and offers educational programs as the solution to social and spiritual problems. To the Baha'i, Jesus is not the incarnation of the one true God. Such a denial is inspired by the spirit of antichrist, according to the Bible (John 1:1-3, 14; I John 4:1-6). The incarnation of Jesus Christ is so foundational to Christianity that any system that denies this truth can, in no way, be compatible with Biblical Christianity.

In 1844, a young Persian (Persia is now Iran), Mirza Ali Muhammed, named himself "the Bab" (the gate). He proclaimed himself as the forerunner of a great teacher to come, and this founded the Baha'i faith. He and his followers were persecuted, and in 1850 the founder was martyred in Tabriz.

Mirza Husayn, follower of "the Bab," announced from exile in Acre, Palestine, that he was the one of whom the founder had spoken. Baha'i recognizes him as the greatest of all the prophets. He established a world headquarters for the faith on Mt. Carmel near Haifa, Israel, and assumed the name "Baha'u'llah." The aim of Baha'i is to unite all religions in to one.

Chapter 11

TM: Relaxation or Religion?

It appears so innocent and is practiced by so many reputable people at all levels of society, but transcendental meditation is one of the most insidious of the cults. Clergymen, priests, nuns, Christians, and Jews practice TM.

There is a vast difference between TM as taught to the public and the real teaching behind TM which is kept secret. Most TM practitioners believe they are involved in a non-religious relaxation technique, which in no way conflicts with their Christian belief. But this is a delusion. The doctrine of TM is pure Hinduism presented in Western terminology. The meditator is gradually drawn into occult bondage and involvement with the spirit world and demonic forces.

A former TM instructor, Dora Gugliotta, observed the many harmful side effects of practicing TM. She tells of emotional breakdowns, symptoms of mental and physical passivity, withdrawal of feelings, marriage breakups, and frightening encounters with demon spirits. TM is deceptive, dangerous, and evil.

Birth of a Cult

Like most cults, there is a dominant personality at the center of the TM movement. His followers are convinced he is an enlightened man and are completely devoted to him. Maharishi Mahesh Yogi, a Hindu monk, is the founder of the TM movement. Born in India in 1918, he graduated from Allahabad University with a B.A. in physics. Subsequently, he became the disciple of a revered holy man, Swami Brahmananda Saraswati, known simply as Guru Dev (divine teacher).

After the death of his master, Maharishi retreated into monastic silence for a few years. He emerged with a determination to teach TM as the solution to mankind's problems. Encouraged by his results, he founded the Spiritual Regeneration Movement (SRM) in India in 1958. He imported TM into the United States in 1959, gaining followers in California.

World Takeover

TM has since grown into a multimillion dollar, worldwide organization. It has vast property holdings, including a TV station, production studios, a large publishing operation, a university (MIU), an electroencephalographic laboratory, various land parcels, resorts, and hundreds of "city academies."

The goal of Maharishi is to win the world for TM. He already claims millions of practitioners and several thousand teachers of TM. TM seeks the respect of governments, the scientific and academic communities, the business world, and the church. There are TM adherents holding influential positions in these and other fields. We have copies of TM's magazine, World Government, which plainly shows the goal of Maharishi Mahesh Yogi.

In 1972, Maharishi launched his "World Plan" to further promote TM. The Science of Creative Intelligence (SCI) is a glossy course that teaches the doctrines of TM using psuedoscientific concepts. It is taught as a credit course in major American universities. SCI concepts are the main propaganda thrust of the World Plan.

The World Plan is administered by the World Plan Executive Council (WPEC). With its "governors" and "ministers," it is beginning to look like a world government in miniature, with Maharishi at its head.

What kind of society would we have if TM were to achieve its goals? Maharishi has said that those who do not meditate are a "drag on society," and "unfit, ignorant and abnormal." In his commentary on the Bhogavad Gita, Maharishi teaches that an enlightened man has a state of consciousness which will justify any action, even allowing him to kill if necessary to support "the purpose of evolution" (*On the Bhagavad Gita*, p. 76). During a public lecture, a TM speaker said that soon everyone in society would be "obliged" to meditate. These are indeed ominous words.

The Big Lie

Transcendental meditation is presented to the public in free introductory lectures, usually held in public libraries or local TM centers. The prospective meditator is told that TM is a simple, natural, mental technique whereby the mind and body gain deep rest. The technique is effortless and anyone can do it. It is practiced twice a day for 20 minutes each time, while sitting comfortably with the eyes closed. TM is not a religion and one does not even have to believe in it for it to be effective. The daily practice of TM will remove stress and help develop mental potential. Thus, the results are improved health, happiness, and more harmonious family and social relationships. Eventually, widespread use of TM, they claim, will lead to world peace.

Scientific studies are used to "prove" the physiological and mental benefits of TM, but these have come into serious question by objective scientists.

The doctrine behind TM appears simple. There are three levels of existence: Action, Thinking, and Being (also called Creative Intelligence or The Absolute). The effortless practice of TM draws the mind to quieter levels of thinking. As the mind goes within, the awareness transcends the thinking process altogether and arrives at Being, the source of all creativity, energy, and intelligence. When one comes out of TM, he is refreshed and maintains the value of Being in daily life. The continued practice of TM leads ultimately to the glorified state of man, known as enlightenment (nirvana).

TM promotes the theory of reincarnation, based on the law that every action has an equal and opposite reaction. If one dies before receiving the full consequences of his actions, he is drawn back into another life. Of course, this teaching is not revealed to the public, but only to those in residence courses for deeper involvement in TM. Obviously, the doctrine of reincarnation is not compatible with the Bible (Hebrews 9:27).

Hinduism in Disguise

The correlation between TM and Hinduism is inescapable. The three major doctrines of Hinduism are:

1. *Karma* — every action (or thought) has an effect that influences the whole world and must return to us.

2. *Samsara* — evolution of the soul toward perfection.

3. *Moksha* — enlightenment or merging with the "Absolute."

These doctrines support reincarnation and pantheism (God is everything). This "god" is the "Absolute" and, since the absolute is within us, we too must be divine. Here again is the humanistic idea that man is his own god. SCI teaches the same concepts in nonreligious terms. By removal of our stresses through the practice of TM, we evolve and realize the Creative Intelligence within ourselves.

Idol Worship

Every potential meditator must first submit to an initiation ceremony. It is said to be an innocent ceremony of thanksgiving to the tradition of TM masters, performed by the teacher. The initiate is only asked to witness it. The ceremony is called a *puja,* which in Sanskrit means "worship." It is chanted in Sanskrit by the TM teacher. The initiate is not aware of the true meaning. He is asked to bring fruit, flowers, and a white handkerchief. The teacher furnishes other items.

The *puja* is performed at a table covered by a white sheet, with a picture of Guru Dev standing in the center. At the foot of the picture is a tray. Around the tray are little bowls of water, rice, sandalpaste, and camphor. On one side is a candle; on the other is incense. The things brought by the initiate are also present. Although the initiate does not know it, the table is an altar, the picture is an icon (idol), and the various items on the table are offerings.

The ceremony consists of three parts. The first is a recitation of the names of deceased Hindu Masters, going back to the Hindu creator-gods, Lord Narayana and Brahma. The middle part consists of offering, in turn, the various items on the table. As each item is offered it is moved to the tray at the foot of the icon, with the refrain, "To the lotus feet of Lord Guru Dev, I bow down." In the third part of the ceremony,

Guru Dev is worshiped as the embodiment of deity! He is called the embodiment of Brahma, Vishnu, and Shiva (the Hindu trinity). At the end of the *puja*, the teacher bows to the icon. He invites the initiate to bow also.

The unwitting participant is clearly involved in worshiping Hindu deities. The spiritual power of these gods is invoked on his behalf. One might ask why Maharishi insists on the ceremony. The deceptive purpose is to psychically link the initiate to the Hindu masters by worship, giving offerings to them, and preparing his mind to receive the mantra.

Idol worship is forbidden in the Bible. This is so important that the first two commandments deal with it: "Thou shalt have no other gods before Me. Thou shalt not make unto thee any graven image: . . . Thou shalt not bow down thyself to them" (Exodus 20:3-5). We are not to invoke other gods or even speak their names (Exodus 23:13).

Mantra and Hindu Gods

At the conclusion of the *puja*, the initiate receives a Sanskrit word called a *mantra*. It is not as meaningless as some think. The initiate is to repeat the mantra silently for 20 minutes, twice daily. This is supposed to bring relaxation and a host of other benefits to the meditator. Like so much in TM, the true meaning of the mantra is kept hidden. Even teachers are strictly forbidden to speak of the *puja* or mantras with one another. TM teachers themselves know little more than what they share with the public.

The meditator is told that his mantra is selected specifically for him. The fact is there are only about 16 mantras. Each one is chosen for a particular age-group. Over the years, Maharishi has shifted the mantras and age-groups around. We are indebted to Miss Dora Gugliotta for much of the information in this chapter. She is a former TM instructor, now converted to Jesus Christ.

The mantras are actually *bija* (seed) names used in the worship of Hindu deities. In his Vedic studies, Maharishi teaches that in Sanskrit, *a word creates its form* because of its vibration at a subtle level of existence. One taps this subtle level in TM. Maharishi says:

"Meditating leads one to contact the gods, thereby gaining their help, and . . . one sins if one does not contact these gods" (*Meditations*, pp. 17, 18; *On the Bhagavad Gita*, p. 201; *Commentary* 3:9-13).

Research into the mantras reveals that Maharishi believes they are not merely names that invoke the power of the deity. *The mantra is the deity itself:* The real (hidden) purpose of meditation is to produce the gradual transformation of the personality of the meditator into that of the deity. As one progresses, he takes on more of the nature of the deity he worships and less of himself. The passivity that results from TM helps this process.

Actually, the gods of Hinduism are demonic spirits against which the Bible warns us. There is no real value in calling their names (by use of the mantra). "There is none other name under heaven given among men, whereby we must be saved . . . [except] Jesus Christ of Nazareth" (Acts 4:10-12). Whether or not we accept the idea that by calling the name of a demon god its form is actually created within, or we simply view the use of the mantra as invoking the demon's presence, the result is the same. The meditator invites satanic influence into his life, and the process can ultimately lead to demonic possession.

TM and Occult Powers

In 1975, Maharishi instituted the TM-Siddhi program. The purpose was to develop the psychic powers such as levitation, ESP, invisibility, and a host of other supernatural feats. Techniques for these abilities are taught, in addition to regular meditation, at a cost of several thousand dollars. Psychic powers are the devil's counterfeit of the gifts of the Spirit bestowed by God on believers.

TM: Another Gospel

"But though we, or an angel from heaven, preach any other gospel unto you than that which we have preached unto you, let him be accursed" (Galatians 1:8). Maharishi declares the "good news" of TM but denies the deity of Jesus; Christ was just an enlightened man. TM denies the necessity of the Cross. "Who is a liar but he that denieth that Jesus is the Christ?'' (I John 2:22).

Christians cannot practice TM and still be right with God: ''Ye cannot drink the cup of the Lord, and the cup of devils: ye cannot be partakers of the Lord's table, and the table of devils'' (I Corinthians 10:21).

Chapter 12

TM Instructor Finds Christ

This is the story of Dora Guggliotfa of Toronto, Ontario Canada.

We met and counseled Dora shortly after she became a Christian and left TM. She is an active lay minister and attends Queensway Cathedral in Toronto. Rev. Ralph Rutlege is her pastor. Dora has been effective in leading many out of the bondage of cults and the occult. Here is her testimony of deliverence from deception.

Transcendental Meditation (TM) promised to be the answer to all my problems. Yet, without realizing it, I was being led deeper into occult bondage.

For six and a half years, TM was my life. Leaving TM was unthinkable. I was convinced it was the most effective path to self-fulfillment and unity with God. Without it, I would still be suffering from the anxiety and depression that plagued me all my life.

At the age of 15, in rebellion, I had rejected God and the Episcopal Church that had been so good to me. After that, all hell broke loose in my mind and I had a nervous breakdown. Life had no meaning for me.

In university I began a pattern of immoral and degrading relationships with men. Later I took drugs searching for mystical experiences. All these years I was a hard-core atheist.

Life was a desperate search for meaning and happiness. Even my psychotherapy was a long and discouraging process. Then I started practicing TM. The first few years were euphoric. All my questions about life were answered, and I felt happier than I'd ever been before. It made me believe in God again.

In order to "evolve" more quickly and gain deeper benefits, I attended a residence course in Spain to become a TM teacher. By this time I was noticing many negative effects of TM, but I was already hooked and did not realize the danger.

My years in TM ended abruptly when God miraculously intervened in my life and I accepted Christ as Saviour.

The practice of TM was introduced to the world in 1959 by Maharishi Mahesh Yogi, a Hindu monk. Since then, Maharishi has developed a multimillion dollar, worldwide organization to evangelize the world for TM. Over 2 million people (1 million in the U.S.) have received instruction in TM. It has infiltrated all levels of society including government and education. In schools and universities it is taught as the Science of Creative intelligence.

It is presented as a simple, mental technique for gaining deep rest by the mind and body. You only need to practice it 20 minutes twice a day. It will not conflict with your own religion because it is not a religion. The benefits are that it improves our minds, keeps us calm and gives us more energy. Our thinking becomes more orderly and our health improves. Our relationships with others improve, and if enough people in the world gain inner peace we would eventually have world peace.

It sounds so innocuous and respectable that even priests and nuns are practicing it as well as ordinary Christians and Jews.

The true nature of TM is disguised with lies and deceit. Every new initiate must attend a ceremony which involves him in idol worshiping. He is told that it's a ceremony of gratitude to the tradition of Hindu masters from which the technique comes. The initiate is only a witness, but he is asked to bring fruit, flowers and a white handkerchief. Other articles such as candles and incense are supplied by the teacher.

The ceremony is chanted in Sanskrit while standing at a table which holds a picture of Guru Dev, Maharishi's dead master. A tray at the foot of the picture receives the items which are offered one by one to the "lotus feet of Guru Dev." The refrain of every offering is "I bow down." The names of the Hindu gods and dead masters of the TM lineage are recited so as to invoke their power and psychically charge the atmosphere. Guru Dev is worshiped as the embodiment of deity. At the end the teacher bows down and invites the initiate to do likewise. Thus, whether he knows it or not, the initiate is involved in the ceremony of worship of Hindu spirits. The ceremony is not only for the TM teacher, it is for the initiate.

This is a clear violation of the first and second commandments, "You shall have no other gods but me. Thous shalt not make to thyself any graven image . . . Thous shalt not bow down to them, nor worship them" (see Exodus 20:3, 4).

The technique of TM involves the mental repetition of a mantra which is said to be a meaningless sound. There are 16 mantras which are selected by age group. The mantra actually is a seed-name of a Hindu deity (demon spirit). At the subtle levels of the mind, the mantra vibration creates the form of the deity. The mantra is the deity itself! The meditation produces the gradual transformation of the personality of the meditator into that of the deity.

What we are doing in TM therefore, is calling on the name of Hindu deity or demon spirit, creating its form and drawing it right into our own being. This is actually inviting demon possession by an act of will. Christians cannot practice TM and expect to retain their salvation.

Hinduism and TM hold the same doctrines in common. The three major doctrines of Hinduism are: 1) Karma — every action has a reaction; 2) Samsara — the evolution of the soul through many lifetimes (reincarnation); 3) Moksha — enlightenment is man's reconciliation with God. Hinduism does not consider itself to be a religion because it considers all religions as part of itself. TM claims that it is not a religion because it is the basis of all religions. Therefore, if TM is not a religion, this is only because it is Hinduism.

Maharishi teaches that Jesus Christ was an enlightened man. We can all become like Him by releasing our stresses through the practice of TM and revealing the divine within. Thus there is no sin, only stress. God is everywhere and in us as well. The impersonal god is revealed in us when we attain enlightenment. This is a humanistic doctrine.

Therefore, TM denies the unique deity of Jesus Christ, who is God in the flesh, and also denies His atoning sacrifice on the cross. The Bible teaches that we are sinners and can only be reconciled to God by accepting in faith Christ's sacrifice to pay for our sins.

After three years as a TM teacher, I was experiencing doubt and confusion about TM. I was always tired, marriages were breaking up, many TM teachers were mentally incompetent and no one seemed to be gaining enlightenment. All areas of my life were falling apart, and I was experiencing more stress and less peace. Mentally I was on the verge of another breakdown. I thought I was going to die.

One night, after I had gone to sleep, another TM teacher called me and told me he had quit TM for Jesus. He quoted a few verses of Scripture which said that Jesus was the only begotten Son of God, and that He was the way, the truth and the life. No one could come to God except by Him.

Instantly, to my horror, I saw that TM was in conflict with Christianity, and I was confronted with a choice. In fear and trembling, I knelt down and turned to Christ. Afterwards, in a frenzy, I purged my home of all my occult articles, rebuking Satan and all his works in the name of Jesus Christ. Now I finally have the peace that passes all understanding and the truth which sets me free.

Chapter 13

Satanism And Witchcraft

The oldest religion in the universe predates the existence of mankind — the angels' worship of Jehovah. Next in antiquity, was the perversion of worship when an angel, exalted in pride, directed worship away from God to himself. Lucifer determined to exalt himself "above the stars [angels] of God." He declared his intention to "be like the Most High [God]." The host of angels that fell with Lucifer in the original rebellion became the first Satan worshipers.

Evil in Eden

The next episode in the history of satanism unfolds in the opening pages of the Bible. Our first parents lived in a paradise and enjoyed communion with God. Into this blissful garden home entered an intruder, Satan, who used a serpent as a medium of communication. In those days the serpent was very different from snakes today. He walked on legs and was a beautiful creature.

The devil never changes his "line": "God is not really God. He's not what He claims to be. Someone else could take His place or be equal to Him." What the devil preached to angels in heaven he repeated to Eve in Eden. First he subtly questioned God's Word: "Yea, hath God said, Ye shall not eat of every tree?" Eve, is it possible you misunderstood God's intention? Surely a loving God would not place any restrictions on you.

Then Satan actually slandered God as a selfish liar: "God doth know that in the day ye eat thereof, then your eyes shall be opened, and ye shall be as gods." God does not want you to have the hidden (occult) knowledge. He wants to keep it to Himself. He is selfish. Finally, he openly denied God's Word: "Ye shall not surely die" (Genesis 3:1-5).

The occult movement is the voice of Satan today. It too questions, then denies, the Word of God: "Surely you are not so narrow as to think that Christ is the only way to God. Partake of our hidden knowledge. Abandon those outdated prohibitions of the Bible. New vistas of awareness await you."

Devil Worship in the Old Testament

When men forsake God, they find another object of worship. In the Old Testament era, God continually urged Israel to forsake the abominations of the heathen who engaged in devil worship and the adoration of demonic idols. Sadly, Israel failed God many times and suffered punishment as a result. They "were mingled among the heathen, and learned their works. And they served their idols; which were a snare unto them. Yea, they sacrificed their sons and daughters unto devils" (Psalm 106:35-37).(See Deuteronomy 32:17; II Chronicles 11:15.)

The apostle Paul equated idolatry with devil worship: "But I say, that the things which the Gentiles sacrifice, they sacrifice to devils" (I Corinthians 10:20). All world religions that make use of idols (such as Hinduism) are demon worship.

Satan in the New Testament

Jesus recognized the reality of the devil. He often cast demons out of the possessed. Paul was followed by a young woman who had an evil spirit of divination until He cast out the demon (Acts 16:16-40). The most outstanding fact about devil worship is revealed in the temptation of Jesus. It seems like madness, but Satan actually asked Jesus to bow and worship him!

Satan's unusual power is revealed in this narrative. Because the Lord allowed it, Satan was able to literally transport Jesus physically and reveal vast and distant scenes to Him in some kind of psychic or visionary display:

"The devil taketh Him up into an exceeding high mountain, and showeth Him all the kingdoms of the world, and the glory of them; and saith unto Him, 'All these things will I give thee, if Thou wilt fall down and worship me'" (Matthew 4:8-9).

Here, as in no other passage, the true desire of the devil is revealed in naked horror. Isaiah and Ezekiel tell of his pride and self-exaltation (Isaiah 14:12-15; Ezekiel 28:12-17), but here is the supreme act of arrogance. His vile intentions are on display: He wants to be God; he wants to be worshiped. All false religions are designed in hell to try to divert worship from the Creator toward the creature. (See Romans 1:18-32.)

Simon Magus

Simon the sorcerer (Acts 8:5-24) was a plague to the Church, according to Early Church fathers who referred to him frequently. (See Justin Martgr Apol. 1, 26.) Evidently, he became a satanic magician or wizard of unusual powers. His colossal ego led him to claim that he was deity himself. Early tradition says Simon became a favorite of the anti-Christian Roman emperor, Nero. He is said to have performed feats of levitation by occult (satanic) power. He founded an order of magicians known as theophites.

Post-Apostolic Era

From early times through the Dark and Middle Ages, satanism continued to find a place in the hearts of benighted mankind. Frequently it took the form of witchcraft, although many witches claim they do not worship Satan. (We will deal with this matter later.)

Knights Templar

The order of the Knights Templar was founded in Palestine, in 1118, as a militant force to protect the Church of the Holy Sepulcher in Jerusalem. After several wars with the Moslem Saracens, the Knights became a powerful organization in control of vast wealth. Whatever the original intention of the movement, it became a foul nest of satanism. Members performed the blasphemous black mass, dabbled in many forms of occultism, and promoted homosexuality.

Manley Hall claims, in his *The Adepts in the Western*

Tradition, that the Templars worshiped a curious deity in the form of a monstrous head, or a demon in the form of a goat named Baphomet, the Goat of Mendes. Hall, an occultist, believes the Templars are part of a secret world conspiracy (the "Illuminati") which will finally become a world government.

Persecution

Satanists and witches went underground, to a great extent, because of persecution. What started as seemingly legitimate prosecution of diabolical satanists became persecution of innocents falsely accused of witchcraft. Many harmless people were killed because they looked or acted strange. To some witch hunters, the existence of a mole or wart on the victim's body was enough to bring accusations of witchcraft!

The Inquisition, begun in 1233 by the Roman Church, was largely superintended by Dominican Friars. Persons charged with witchcraft were tortured until they confessed — then put to death or imprisoned. During the 16th century over 30,000 were executed in France during the reign of Henry III.

The "bible" of the inquisitors was *Malleus Maleficarum* ("Hammer of the Witches"), written by two priests, Sprenger and Kramer in 1486. It was a chief cause of the witch hunts that continued into the 16th century.

Queen Elizabeth was responsible for the Witchcraft Act of 1563. In 1601 her successor, James I, introduced an even more severe law. Under these laws many who were not witches suffered loss of property, imprisonment, and death. The last of the witch laws was repealed by Great Britain in 1951. This signaled a new age of toleration, and a revival of witchcraft and satanism has resulted.

The Hell Fire Club

Powerful political influence was wielded by the Hell Fire Club in 18th century England. It was organized by Sir Francis Dashwood, a member of Parliament. Dashwood performed black masses, in which a nude woman served as the altar, in order to summon up the power of evil spirits to serve his diabolical aims. Daniel Mannix's book, *The Hell Fire Club,* states that it was dedicated to black magic, sexual orgies, and political conspiracies.

Adam Weishaupt and the Illuminati

Weishaupt was a Satan worshiper. In 1776, he started a secret organization known as the "Illuminati," for the purpose of promoting political intrigue and, ultimately, a world government. His people infiltrated the extremist Jacobin Free Mason lodges of France, and to them is attributed the cause of the bloody French Revolution. Some of Weishaupt's followers were Voltaire, Mirabeau, and Robespierre. Basilea Schlenk says:

"Nowadays his objective is being openly proclaimed in satanism — the overthrow of the government through revolutions and chaos — both communism and satanism are fed by the same source of inspiration — hatred of Christ and Christians" (*The Eve of Persecution*, a tabloid).

The Man Who Called Himself Antichrist

Aliester Crowley, who died in 1947, was called "the most evil man in the world" by his critics. He called himself "the beast of revelation." His own mother said he was the Antichrist. Crowley headed a group called the Golden Dawn, which was dedicated to demonism, political intrigue, drug usage, demonism, and sexual perversion. His life-style was bizarre, and on one occasion he branded a mistress with the number 666 (Revelation 13:18). A prolific writer, he influenced many toward satanism and the occult.

Hitler and Satan

Numerous European writers have dealt with the idea that Hitler was involved in occult satanism. During his early years in Vienna, Hitler eagerly devoured the occult and anti-Semitic outpourings of *Ostara* magazine. He learned many occult mysteries from the editor of *Ostara*. Later Hitler was introduced into satanism by Dietrich Eckart, one of seven founders of the Nazi party and a dedicated worshiper of Satan and practitioner of black magic. The Nazi party had a Federal Commissary for Occultism.

Indeed, Hitler was one of the outstanding antichrists of our times. His knowledgeable involvment in the occult adds to our understanding of this monster who was responsible not only for the slaughter of Jews, but also for the 50 million casualties of World War II. Further studies reveal Hitler understood the Biblical concept and wanted to be the Antichrist. For further reading, see such books as: *Morning of the Magicians*, by Louis Pauwels and Jacques Bergier[Briarcliff Manor, N.Y.: Stein & Day, 1964]; *The Occult and the Third Reich*, by Jean Michael Angebert [New York: Macmillan Pub. Co., 1964]; *Spear of Destiny*, by Trevor Ravenscroft. *The Twisted Cross* by Joseph J. Carr [Huntington House, 1985.]

Current Revival of Satanism

Both satanism and witchcraft have enjoyed a revival since the latter part of the 19th century. They have gained a certain respectability and a new image. Many high schools and colleges now offer courses in witchcraft and magic. Isaac Bonewits was granted the first Doctor of Philosophy in magic (Berkeley University). He is a leader in the occult revival of modern times.

Church of Satan

Anton Szandor LaVey founded the Satanist Church on Walpurgisnacht, April 30, 1966. Walpurgisnacht is a major festival on the calandar of witches. LaVey now appears to have about 20,000 dues-paying members in the United States.

LaVey has claimed that Satan is not a person. Rather, he represents the natural force that men can tap and use for their own ends — sort of like "the force" in the *Star Wars* movie. Most devil worshipers believe in the reality of Satan. LaVey seems to contradict himself in the introduction of his *Satanic Bible:*

"What amuses us most is that you indicate that a mere command to Satan in Jesus' name is sufficient to dismiss him. The Prince of Darkness regards both God and Jesus Christ as insignicant figments of man's more infantile imagination."

LaVey's Church of Satan is only the visible tip of the iceberg. Most serious satanists try to keep their activities secret.

The Black Mass

Satanists and witches blaspheme Christ in the black mass, a blatant attack on the Lord's Supper. Satan is the object of worship (witches substitute "the horned god"). He is represented by an obscene figure of Christ and/or a goat. Black candles and a chalice of blood add a touch of the macabre. A nude woman is usually the altar. Sex orgies climax the rite. Some sacrifice a human baby and use its blood in the chalice. The black mass is usually performed in the nude. Recent *Time* magazine articles leave no doubt that these ceremonies are being commonly — if secretly — practiced all over America.

We counseled a young woman who had been a satanic priestess. She fled the cult when the high priest (her brother) wanted to sacrifice her baby. She was living in hiding and feared for her life. Later the church that helped her was fire-bombed, although there is no conclusive proof of who did it.

Black and White

Witches claim there are two kinds of magic; white magic for blessing and good, black for evil and cursing. We have seen specialty stores in the United States, Mexico, and Canada selling philters — potions, charms, and occult paraphernalia — for the practice of both kinds of magic.

The word *witchcraft* is derived from *wicca*, an old Anglo-Saxon word meaning "a magician who weakens the power of evil." The idea is that the witch summons supernatural, and even evil spirit beings, to do his bidding. The witch stands inside a pentagram (star-shaped symbol) for protection from the evil entity called up by incantation and chanting. Many witches deny the existence of either Satan or God. They worship a female goddess, the "all mother," or the old horned one, Baphomet, the Goat of Mendes. Whatever they call their god, it is still the devil. God does not differentiate between white and black magic. It is all forbidden (Deuteronomy 18:10-12).

Which Was First?

Wicca is called "the old religion." Witches boast that witchcraft is far older than Christianity. This is a vain boast since the earliest worship on record is that of angels for Jehovah. The worship of God was practiced by Adam in Eden. It is expanded in the Old Testament and brought to fulfillment in Jesus. Following the Ascension, Christianity was born as the ongoing expression of God's progressive revelation to man, not as a new religion. (See Hebrews 1:1.)

Boasting of Evil

Once it was a disgraceful thing to be called a witch, but now people openly boast of their evil. (See II Timothy 3:1-8.) In her book, *Diary of a Witch* (New York: New American Library, 1972), Sybil Leek boasts, "I am a witch." She tells of the influence the occultist Aliester Crowley had on her life. She recalls his telling her grandmother: "This is the one who will take up where I leave off . . . She'll live to see occultism almost being understood."

Since most witch covens (groups of 13 participants) meet in secret, it is hard to estimate their numbers, but evidence indicates covens operate in almost every city, town, and village. Ron Held writes that there are 3 million satanists in Germany alone.

Witch youth Outreach

"Witch Cult Survives to Present Day" heads a full-page article in an official high school newspaper in our files. The article features a photo of Alex Sanders, "King of the Witches." The conclusion states:

"Witchcraft affords a fascinating glimpse into another world; but for those who are drawn to the supernatural, who are prepared to devote time and trouble to it, witchcraft offers no less than the *power to achieve a new dimension of life*." [Italics mine.]

Many teen magazine articles promote witchcraft. *Ingenue Magazine* offers "Friendly Witchcraft." The author says:

"There are spells for almost every occasion. For the girl who doesn't have time to wait for a candle to burn down there's a less time-consuming possibility. Touch the hand of the boy with your hand and say, 'Bestarberto corrumpit viscerus ejus hominum' (which means, "Bestarberto entices the inner man.') That's all there is to it. He's enchanted."

The reader is urged to visit a witchcraft museum and read suggested books.

In *Loving Fashions Magazine* an article is titled "How to Be a Witch." Young readers are assured:

"If you are interested in becoming a modern young witch
. . . read the following instructions. They are not made up.
They come from a six-month study of witchcraft manuals."

Teenset Magazine explains:

"Understanding the significance of serious magic requires
study, empathy. . . . The men and women who practice and
believe in the black arts are not comical figures to be scoffed
and laughed at; moreover they view their beliefs with the same
force of conviction as any Christian priest."

Who Will Win?

She walked purposefully down the aisle of the Ohio church
in which I had just ministered. I noticed she was wearing an
ankh, an Egyptian occult symbol of life. She said: "You were
mostly right tonight. I too believe in the second coming of
Jesus, and that there will be an Armageddon. But, preacher,
my god, not yours is going to win. I know you serve Jesus but
my god is Lucifer, and he will destroy your God. You poor
sleepy Christians only half hear what you say. They only
half believe their own Bible, but we satanists are dedicated
to our cause and we will win over you."

I said: "Lady, you are wrong. I do not know what kind of
Christians you have been around, but most of the ones I know
are awake and really believe the Bible. You are in one of
the last-days revival churches tonight. This is not a modernist
church. Some of the most alert people in the world are right
here tonight. You had better read the last pages of the Bible,
because there you will find out who is going to win."

The Bible predicts the rise of occultism and devil worship
in the end times (I Timothy 4:1). It also tells of the doom of
those who follow the devil. (See Revelation 20:7-15.)

Chapter 14

A Matter Of Life And Death

Death is a mystery. The materialistic view that termination of physical life is the final end does not satisfy. It is no wonder that satanic attempts to deceive in this area are strong. The Bible teaches survival of the soul and ultimate resurrection of the body. If I die as the person I am, I will live again in this body — resurrected and glorified.

Recycling of Souls

Once the domain of Eastern mystics, reincarnation is now widely believed in the western world. The concept is that after death the soul returns in another life form, perhaps a human, an animal, a tree, or any living thing. Hindus will not eat meat for fear of devouring an ancestor! Obviously, one cannot believe in both reincarnation and resurrection. Why do so many believe in reincarnation?

Bridey Murphy

An alleged proof of reincarnation is hypnotic regression, a process in which a hypnotist puts the subject in a trance, and suggests the person is going back in time to remember past experiences. Childhood memories are revived and, if the session is "successful," even past lives are remembered.

In the 1950's, Morey Bernstein published a book, *The Search for Bridey Murphy* (Garden City, N.Y.: Doubleday & Co., 1965), describing his hypnosis of a Colorado housewife.

She recalled her previous life as Bridey Murphy in Ireland from 1798 to 1866. Although she was not a history student, the tape-recorded sessions revealed Mrs. Simmons displayed an extensive knowledge of 19th century Cork County and Belfast. Other even more convincing cases of regression seem to prove reincarnation. How is the Christian to interpret these cases?

Lying Spirits

Satan's purpose is to deceive concerning the nature of death, afterlife, and judgment. In both reincarnation and spiritism (communication with the dead), we see the work of "familiar spirits" (Leviticus 19:31; 20:6). These demonic spirits are knowledgeable and can easily impersonate the dead. Francis Schaffer points out that this endless system of "rebirths" (in reincarnation) leaves man without purpose and utterly alone in a meaningless universe.

The Bible, however, reveals men's fall and subsequent brokenness, and offers redemption and a meaningful relationship with God through Jesus Christ, who alone brings purpose to life. Search the writings of the Bhagavad-Gita, the Vedas, or other books of the East; you will never find anything as satisfying as Jesus.

The Sleeping Prophet

The Association for Research and Enlightenment, founded on the teachings of the late Dr. Edgar Cayce, is a fast-growing occult movement. The A.R.E. is representative of cults teaching reincarnation in the United States. I researched the movement at its headquarters in Virginia Beach, Virginia. A young lady had told me, "Edgar Cayce was a Christian leader. He read the Bible, taught Sunday school, and spoke highly of Jesus." This young lady's statement and her involvement in the A.R.E. led me to do my "on-location" research.

Truth From a Trance?

Cayce is called the sleeping prophet because his methods involved self-hypnosis. While in this trance state, Cayce gave readings, teachings, prophecies, and analyses for healing. I delved into volumes of stenographic records containing thousands of trance readings given by Dr. Cayce. I was allowed to photograph any pages I desired. Indeed, Cayce spoke about Jesus, but his "Yeshua" is not the Jesus of the Gospels. His "Jesus" as the 14th reincarnation of Adam, who had, at various times, been Joshua, the father of Zoroaster, and finally "Yeshua of Nazareth." Cayce's "Jesus" was not the uniquely virgin-born Son of God, but merely one of many masters who have appeared throughout the ages.

Once To Die

The A.R.E. librarian was most helpful. At one point I asked her if she had considered what the Bible teaches about life after death. I mentioned Hebrews 9:27: "It is appointed unto men once to die, but after this the judgment." She responded: "Mr. Lewis, you will get confused if you read the Bible. I personally stick to the teachings of Dr. Cayce, and books about him."

I continued: "I don't want to confuse you, but when Moses appeared on the Mount of Transfiguration with Jesus (Mark 9) he was still Moses even though he had been dead for centuries. He had not gone through identity change after identity change. This disproves reincarnation."

Christian or Pagan?

Many think the A.R.E. is a Christian organization. This seems to be the image they are trying to project. In reality, the A.R.E. is a syncretic movement; they are trying to combine all world religions into one common philosophy. One can be a member of the A.R.E. if he believes in any god concept and agrees with the basic purposes of the cult.

Talking to the Dead

Spiritualism is the practice of [allegedly] communicating with the dead. Essential to such activity is the "medium" who has a "spirit guide," known, in the Bible, as a "familiar spirit" (Isaiah 19:3).

The late Episcopalian bishop, James Pike, was convinced he had communicated with his dead son who had shot and killed himself on February 4, 1966. Knowing of the strange ideas of Bishop Pike, I wanted to meet him personally. I found him at the meeting of the House of Bishops in Seattle's City Center. When I asked for an interview, he graciously consented. In response to my questions, he confirmed his rejection of Biblical inspiration and the miraculous nature of Jesus. When Dennis Bennett, a charismatic Episcopalian minister, was mentioned Pike said, "I know Dennis and his Pentecostalism — and I want none of it."

While Pike rejected the supernaturalism of the Bible and the current work of the Holy Spirit, he accepted the realm of the psychic. He believed he had communicated with his dead son through mediums Arthur Ford and Ena Twigg.

Modern Spiritualism

Most historians date the founding of modern spiritualism at March 31, 1848. Two young girls, Margaret and Kate Fox, of Hydesville, New York, began to receive communications from a spirit that claimed to be Charles Rosna. The "ghost" was that of a peddler who had been murdered by a previous tenant of the house the Foxes lived in. Many writers say the whole thing was a fraud, but Sir Arthur Conan Doyle and others were convinced it was real.

Spiritualism continues to grow steadily, adding members to its ranks throughout the world. There are even Christian Spiritualist Churches represented by organizations like the Greater World Christian Spiritualist League which claims over 500 churches. Their doctrinal system does not include a Biblical plan of salvation. While some texts are cited, there is very little Biblical truth.

Fraud or Reality?

One of America's former leading mediums (now converted) told me that while he had made many spirit contacts, none were spirits of the dead, but impersonations by his demonic familiar spirit. There are two levels of fraud in spiritualism. One is perpetrated by the medium using trickery. The other is fraudulent activity produced by evil spirits. M Lamar Keene, author of *The Psychic Mafia*, (New York: Dell Publishing Co., 1977), claims that almost all spiritualists are fraudulent (as he was), but that some have real supernatural powers. The Bible treats the subject seriously and from its teaching we conclude that contacts can be explained as demonic manifestations.

There are two kinds of mediums. A trance medium is one who goes into an unconscious state and the ghost of the dead person, supposedly, speaks through the medium's lips. Other mediums exude a wispy substance called ectoplasm which takes the form of the dead person who is seeking to communicate.

In reality, however, contact is not with ghosts of the dead but with familiar spirits. The Bible forbids such communications with demons (Deuteronomy 18:9-15; Isaiah 8:19). When King Saul sought the witch of Endor (I Samuel 28), it was God, not the witch, that brought Samuel from the dead to condemn Saul for this evil. The witch herself was terrified when Samuel, and not her familiar spirit, appeared. She knew her powers had nothing to do with this. Saul's tragic seance brought the punishment of death to him (I Chronicles 10:13-14).

Where Are the Dead?

The Bible describes the state of the dead. They are conscious. The wicked are in hell, and the righteous are with the Lord (Luke 16:19-23; II Corinthians 5:8). There was a change when Jesus was resurrected. We will see our loved ones in eternity, but we are not to seek contact with the dead now. Attempts to do so can lead to demonic possession or harassment.

The warning given by Isaiah is very explicit:

"When men tell you to consult mediums and spiritists, who whisper and mutter, should not a people inquire of their God? Why consult the dead on behalf of the living? To the law and to the testimony! If they do not speak according to this word, they have no light of dawn. . . . They will be thrust into utter darkness" (Isaiah 8:19, 20, 22, *New International Version*).

Why seek counsel from the dead when you have access to the living God?

Thanatology

Thanatology, the science of death, is the newest spiritist

deception. Raymond Moody's popular book, *Life After Life* (New York: Bantam Books, 1976), relates the experiences of people who have "died" and come back to life. Moody, who has a long history in the occult, describes a journey into death as going through a long, dark tunnel. At the end, one is met by a "being of light" who helps evaluate the person's past life and prepares him for the next step of cosmic evolution. Biblical ideas of judgment are replaced with a new view, not of "judgment, but rather cooperative development towards the ultimate end of self realization.

The problem is complicated by the fact that there are valid testimonies in existence of Christians who have actually died and revived, and tell of marvelous contact with Jesus — not Moody's being of light who reminds us of Satan appearing as an angel of light (II Corinthians 11:14).

There is a need for literature to help those who counsel the dying. Unfortunately, some pastors have filled this void with non-Christian books on thanatology. Dr. Elizabeth Kubler-Ross' book, *Death: The Final Stage of Growth* (Englewood Cliffs, NJ: Prentice-Hall, 1975), does not reveal her spiritualist inclinations. However, it is no secret that she has long been deeply involved in the occult. She has a "spirit guide" named Salem. She believes she lived in Jesus' time as "Isabel." Her San Diego retreat, Shanti-Nilaya, shares facilities with the Church of the Facet of Divinity, a cult that promotes sexual involvement with alleged materialized spirit beings (*Time Magazine*, November 12, 1979, European Edition). For a full treatment of thanatology order the April, 1977 Spiritual Counterfeits Project Journal. Write Spiritual Conterfeits Project, Box 4308, Berkeley, CA 94704.

At the Movies

The film *Beyond and Back* presents a strange mixture of "Christian" ideas along with an examination of the psychic, seances, mediums, and spiritism — all as evidence for life after death. Produced by a Mormon-controlled company, it presents a Universalist-occult view. (See Radix Tabloid, October-November, 1978 for a review. Available from SCP; Box 4308, Berkeley, CA 94704. Send $2.00).

Resurrection

The Bible teaches survival after death. The Lord will bring the souls in heaven back with Him at the time of the Rapture (I Thessalonians 4:13-18). Their bodies will be resurrected and glorified. In I Corinthians 15:35-57, Paul explains the resurrection. Even if a body is burned, God will bring that body back together again and make it new. "God giveth it a body as it hath pleased Him, and to every seed His own body" (I Corinthians 15:38). Believe me, if our future new bodies will please God, they will also please us. Hallelujah!

Chapter 15

The Road To Endor

After Rudyard Kipling read the story of King Saul and the witch of Endor (I Samuel 28), he wrote:

The Road to Endor is the oldest road,
And the craziest road of all.
Straight it leads to the witch's abode.
As it did in the days of Saul.
And nothing has changed of the sorrow in store
For those who go down the road to Endor.

An article in *McCall's* magazine, "The Age of Occult," asks: "Housewives hold seances, gurus speak on college campuses, businessmen exploit the zodiac, scientists investigate ESP. Where in the world can the Age of Aquarius be taking us?" Our answer: It leads down the old road to Endor, the way of spiritual tragedy (I Chronicles 10:13-14; Isaiah 47:9-14).

The Choice Is Yours

You are free to choose whatever religion you wish to pursue, but no one should delude himself into thinking that occult practices such as tarot cards, astrology, palm reading, fortune-telling, psychic healing, spirit writing, Ouija boards, aura balancing, magic, and a host of other evil practices are in any way compatible with Biblical Christianity. If you want God's guidance you must not dabble with Satan's false guidance (I Corinthians 10:21).

Many Christians are snared by the devil because some occult activity looks so innocent ("it's only a game"), or the end result (healing, guidance) seems so desirable.

A lady strongly protested my outspoken analysis of the occult. After the service she came to me and said: "You are completely narrow-minded. We have been members of this church for 15 years, and I want you to know that we go to a psychic healer every Monday night. He tunes up our psyche and gives us healing. What's the difference if we get healing from him, or if the pastor prays for us and we get it from Jesus?" I told her the difference has to do with where you want to spend eternity.

Comics, Games, and Toys

Each Christmas season sees the introduction of more and more psychic toys and games for children and adults. Electronic hypnotizing machines, crystal balls, mystic pyramids, divining rods, alpha and beta brain-wave control machines, ESP communicators, and scores of others are now offered. One chain gift store offers a voodoo doll kit with hexes, spells, and instructions. The occult is packaged to look like "fun." Pastors report a definite increase in the number of children needing deliverance from occult bondage and oppression.

A recent comic strip depicted a formerly lame boy going to a "white witch" for his deliverance from a demon. Dondi was delivered by witchcraft. TV cartoons offer a psychic feast weekly. Comic books explore every aspect of spiritism. School libraries have books on the occult in children's language. *Read Magazine* for the classroom defines various occult and ESP phenomena and tells the story of psychic experiences. Some children even get involved in levitation experiments, communication with the dead, and hypnotism.

Celebrating With Demons

Witches celebrate four major holidays: February 2, Candlemas; April 30, Walpurgisnacht or Roodmas; August 1, Lammas; and October 31, Holloween. Dorine Ervine, a converted English witch, is amazed that some churches celebrate the satanic holiday Halloween. She vividly recalls making jokes with her fellow witches and mocking Christians who had parties on Halloween. The seemingly harmless fun of "trick or treat" comes from the Middle Ages when, if you did not "treat" the witches, they would cast a spell (curse) on you.

If a youth group wants a fall fun activity, why not celebrate the Biblical feast of Sukkoth (Feast of Tabernacles) — the rejoicing for the harvest? Call your local Jewish rabbi for the date of Sukkoth. Why not have a joint activity with the Jewish youth of the synagogue to explore your mutual heritage?

Growing Involvement

A *National Enquirer* poll indicates that about 50 percent of people believe in the occult. The percentage is higher an ong women than among men. It's higher in the 18 to 29-year-old bracket. Also the higher the income, the higher the ratio. More whites than blacks accept the occult, the incidence of belief is higher in the western United States, and college graduates outrank those with less education. These statistics cited and analyzed by Rene Noorbergen in *The Soul Hustlers* (Grand Rapids: Zonderian Publishing House, 1976). Noorbergen formerly did a favorable biography of Jean Dixon, but has since changed his mind about her and the entire psychic realm.

Starstruck

Two businessmen were about to form a partnership. One of them said, "I want to consult my attorney about some final details before we sign the contracts."

The other said, "Fine, that will give me time to consult my astrologer for his advice."

It is not at all unusual for businessmen, politicians, doctors, and housewives to seek the advice of astrologers to guide them. They believe that the motions and positions of the stars, sun, moon, and planets can provide knowledge of the future or a given course of action.

Astrology is the most popular form of occult activity. Over 1200 daily newspapers feature horoscope columns which are read by over 40 million people in the United States. It is estimated there are about 10,000 full-time and 175,000 part-time astrologers. In 350 department stores from coast to coast, an estimated 30,000 customers a month receive "personalized" horoscopes or "psychoastrological portraits" from IBM computers via Zodiatronic service system.

What Is Astrology?

Based on ancient pagan worship of the stars and planets as gods, the system of astrology came into its own in Babylon. The theory of astrology can be stated in fairly simple terms. The zodiac or heavens is that portion of the sky through which the sun, moon, and planets "move" from east to west. The zodiac is divided into 12 parts or "houses." Each house is named for a constellation of stars. These are the 12 signs of the zodiac. The 12 constellations or signs pass through each of the 12 houses each year. The sun, moon, and planets pass through the houses every 24 hours.

A zodiacal sign is assigned to each person, depending on the time of year he was born. This astrological sign is supposed to determine his character and destiny. The position of the heavenly bodies at any given time can, allegedly, be used to forecast a person's immediate and future lot in life.

Astrology has been refuted both scientifically and Biblically. The system is based on an earth-centered universe, but the solar system is sun-centered — not earth-centered. In addition, the position of the constellations has shifted about 30 degrees in the last 2,000 years, which means a Virgo is now actually a Libra, a Libra is now a Scorpio, and so on. However few astrologers take this into account. Other flaws are outlined by Kenneth Boa in *Cults, World Religions, and You* (Wheaton, IL: Victor Books, 1977).

Astrology and the Word of God

Our final authority is the Word of God, and it strongly condemns astrology. Forbidden are the activities of "observers of times" (astrologers) (Deuteronomy 18:14). Isaiah scorns those who listen to the astrologers:

"Let now the astrologers, the stargazers, the monthly prognosticators, stand up, and save thee. . . . Behold, they . . . shall not deliver themselves" (Isaiah 47:13-14).

Numerous Scripture passages speak of the vanity of the "Host of heaven" (Jeremiah 8:1-2; 19:13; Zephaniah 1:4-6).

Jean Dixon

One of America's best known astrologers, Jean Dixon, is well-known for her varied psychic talents. I have seen her make predictions by reading vibrations from an individual's fingertips. I heard her predict trouble for Ted Kennedy involving "a body of water," in October 1968, months before the Chappaquiddick tragedy.

I asked Mrs. Dixon in a public meeting, "Do you believe in the literal return of Jesus?"

She said, "Oh yes, I do believe. I believe a *mighty power* will arise in Jerusalem and unite the Jews, Moslems, and Christians. Everyone will bow and worship this mighty power."

That is a prophecy of the Antichrist if I ever heard one! (See II Thessalonians 2:4; Revelation 13:8.).

Mrs. Dixon tells of a vision given her on July 14, 1952. A serpent came and gazed into her eyes. In the serpent's eyes "was all the knowing wisdom of the ages." On February 5, 1962, another vision revealed the birth of a male child who will create a world religion and a world government, and will receive worship from all men. Again, the Antichrist — although she did not recognize him. She said he would be the founder of a new Christianity. All the evidence indicates Jean Dixon's talent is occult — not Christian or Biblical.

Outer Space Connection

Mrs. Dixon says she is in contact via mental telepathy with the occupants of UFOs. They will land in the near future and contact our government. Many other psychics agree. Earth's salvation from famine, war, and energy crises will be brought by our "space brothers."

I have interviewed and corresponded with many people who claim to have had contact with alien beings in UFOs. In every case, the person has had previous involvement in Eastern mysticism, metaphysics, or some form of demonism. Never have I met a born-again Christian who has had a direct contact. I have met many Christians who have seen UFOs, but never one who has had a "close encounter of the third kind" — unless it was prior to conversion. And those who did experience a contact before conversion attribute it to demonic delusion!

Most evangelical writers conclude that UFOs are real and have a physical manifestation, but are delusive and demonic origin. (See *UFOs What on Earth Is Happening* by Weldon and Levitt.)

Exodus From Obsession

A new Christian asked why he could not get rid of satanic influence in his life. When I inquired about his previous religious background, I discovered he and his wife were involved in Eckankar readings, spirit writing, astral projection (sending the soul out of the body), and other occult practices. When I visited their home I found a room full of occult appliances, games, and books. When Paul had a revival at Ephesus, the people burned all their books on the "curious [Psychic] arts" (Acts 19:19). When all the books and appliances were burned, liberation came to these new Christians too.

Miss Dora Gugliotta was a TM instructor and occultist. After her conversion she experienced continual demonic harassment until she threw out all her occult books and devices. She told us now her motto is: "When in doubt, throw it out!" Those who have been involved in the occult must repudiate the demonic practices that gripped them if they want true liberty in Jesus Christ. Refuse Satan's guidance systems. To even read a horoscope (for fun or curiosity) is to expose one's self to the devil's influence.

True Guidance

"For as many as are led by the Spirit of God, they are the sons of God" (Romans 8:14). Why look for a psychic bag of tricks when you can go directly to the true and living God for guidance? Better than advice from the stars is light from the One who is "the bright and morning star" (Revelation 22:16).

Chapter 16

Reaching The Cultist With The Gospel

The cults both pose a problem and represent a positive challenge to the church. We must always be wary of infiltration, lest "wolves in sheep's clothing" rob from the flock of God. Our on-guardedness, however, should not blind us to the fact that the cults are a mission field. We despise untruths and deception, but we love those who have been ensnared by Satan's lies, and long to bring them to our Lord, Jesus Christ.

Importance of the Word

Our program is two-fold. On one hand, we must educate our own people in sound Biblical and theological concepts. The importance of good doctrine is emphasized in many passages of Scripture. (See John 7:16-17; Acts 2:42; 5:28; I Timothy 1:10; 4:6, 13, 16; 5:17; 6:3; II Timothy 3:10, 16; 4:2-3; Titus 1:9; 2:1, 7, 10.) Doctrine simply means teaching. According to the Bible, our Christian walk is not complete without correct doctrine.

It is appalling that many people who have been in church for years are unable to give an adequate Biblical explanation of the Trinity, the deity of Christ, or the person of the Holy Spirit. It is not enough to simply express a belief in these things; we must also be "set for the defense of the Gospel" (Philippians 1:7). (See also I Peter 3:15; Jude 3.)

Ronald Enroth is chairman of the Sociology Department at Westmont College in Santa Barbara, California, and the author of *Youth, Brainwashing, and the Extremist Cults* (Grand Rapids: Zondervan Publishing House, 1977). He wrote:

"Lack of theological understanding is sadly true of many Christian young people. . . . Their superficial knowledge of the Bible and a lack of systematic grounding in their faith leave them wide open for the cults" *(Christian Herald)*.

Enroth points out that unequipped youth are especially vulnerable to groups like the Way, The Bible Speaks, The Walk, The Local Church, and others that can seemingly overwhelm with their Bible knowledge. There is no substitute for II Timothy 2:15!

Searching Souls

People are in the cults because they are looking for something — often, the truth. Others are seeking peace, security, or a sense of self-esteem. With this in mind, we can assume that the Word of God will have a powerful effect as we share our faith with the cult member. We have seen many bound souls coming to Christ in our Bible conferences on the cults and the occult. And Christians are leading cultists to Christ through effective personal witnessing. While it is difficult to reach people in some of the cults, it is not impossible.

The purpose of our emphasis on correct doctrine is to strengthen the faith of those who are already saved, not for argumentation with the cultist. Later we will discuss why argumentation is not very effective. In witnessing to the cult members, simply use whatever you do know of the Word and your testimony. When Dora Gugliotta, an ex-TM teacher got saved it was because a brand-new convert had phoned her and quoted three simple Scripture verses to her. This led to her conversion and deliverance from TM, aura balancing, and other occult practices. Of course, you must study the Word and sound doctrine, but do not wait until you have achieved mastery to begin witnessing.

We live in a strange age. On one hand, there are atheists who do not believe God exists and, on the other hand, occultists who seem ready to believe anything. Actually, the occultist is easier to reach than the atheist or the intellect-tripping cultist (such as Jehovah's Witnesses). I spent 3½ years in dialogue with one atheist before any progress could be seen. But we have seen many occultists saved when they recognized the superiority of Jesus. They had already been seeking the truth and believed in the supernatural, so when Jesus was presented, the Holy Spirit convicted them and conversion resulted.

Love Is the Key

Some people make fun of cultists. Others like to "witness" because they enjoy arguing. These people are missing the essential ingredient of *love*. We must expose cultic error, but we must do it in the spirit of love; otherwise, we are a "tinkling cymbal" (I Corinthians 13). I have never seen a person won to God through anger.

Are you willing to befriend the cult member? Are you willing to listen attentively to him? Many cultists urgently need, and seek, acceptance — which is why they joined the cult in the first place. By listening to his story, you will find out why and how the person got involved. This will give you needed information so you can be the channel through which the healing of Christ can flow.

Satan is always trying to destroy people. He works through the circumstances in an individual's life. This is why you must discover all you can about the person's background and motivations. It is better to get into a discussion of beliefs only after the friendship is established and his confidence is won. God will open the doors so you can ask about his salvation and relationship with God.

You may be surprised to find the cults are "love"-oriented. But it is a false love. It does not lead to liberty but to bondage and slavery. The cultist may have a false sense of love, peace, and tranquility. People in cults frequently come from problem situations and are looking for something to give stability to their lives. The cult, centered on a strong personality and built on a strong ideology that is continually drilled into its members, offers all of this to its devotees.

Loss of Face

For the cultist to admit he is wrong entails great "loss of face." The cult member is not easily argued or talked out of his beliefs. He will not submit to coercion. He is already deeply religious. In many cases he has burned his bridges behind him; he has abandoned his job, parents, friends, church, and society. You can expect him to be antagonistic when leaving the cult is suggested. He cannot reconvert without loss of esteem. He believes he already has the truth and you are in error. Your brand of Christianity is inferior to what he has. It gives him status and prestige in his own eyes. The cultist is aware of the shortcomings of the church and will point these out to you. He has already had to endure ridicule and rejection — he knows how to handle them. But if he senses genuine love and concern in you, this may be the one thing that will break down all the barriers Satan has erected.

He Came Not to Condemn

We must avoid condemning the cultist as a person. Avoid any indication that Christians consider him "loony" or ignorant. Remember, your offensive is against false teaching, not the person. Beware of the temptation to win arguments to satisfy your own ego.

Learn to use what Ed Decker calls "third-person witnessing." This separates the cultist from the line of attack. For example, do not say: "You are really mixed up!" or, "You sure are in error!" Instead say: "I have considered the teachings of your group, and I have a problem with Joseph Smith's teaching about the nature of God." You would then go on to contrast Smith's Mormon teaching with what the Bible says. By using this approach, you place the burden on yourself. This allows the cultist to answer without losing his self-esteem. You can use the same scriptural arguments, but you will not be attacking the person.

Confronting Satan's Power

Frequently the cultist cannot break free until deliverance from demonic force is obtained. Those who witness for the Lord should not seek demonic confrontation, but they may find it is sometimes unavoidable. It is no accident that Paul refers to religious error as "doctrines of devils" (I Timothy 4:1).

While I was preaching on deliverance from occult bondage some time ago, a young woman began to scream, "Help me, help me, help me!" Then her voice changed from a high-pitched scream to a gutteral growl. It was so terrifying that one lady ran out of the meeting. The tormented girl's face contorted and her features became grotesque. Then she fell under the pews, writhing and screaming.

I calmly told the people that God had everything under control (even though it didn't seem like it), and asked everyone to pray. I went to the girl and commanded the demon to be silent and let her exercise her own will. When I told the young woman to open her eyes, she looked around in bewilderment. I asked her name and if she knew where she was, She spoke slowly and seemed confused, "I guess . . . well, I think I'm in a church." It was the first time she had been in an evangelical church. She had an occult background. When I asked her if she wished to be free from the awful power that bound her, she replied tearfully, "Oh, yes! More than anything else in the world!"

That awful demonic power began to manifest itself again. But it left at once when we rebuked it on the authority of God's Word, in the name of the Lord Jesus Christ. The girl accepted Christ as her Saviour. She is now married to a fine young Christian man and is serving the Lord. This is a well-documented case, with many witnesses. The church service was being taped when the incident occured, and the entire episode was recorded.

I don't go looking for demons, and people who do make me uncomfortable. But when a confrontation with satanic powers occurs, Jesus always provides the wisdom and power to deal with them for the glory of God and the deliverance of souls.

Infiltration

We must be watchful in these end times, for a battle of spiritual powers is taking place. Sharon Harrington had once been a satanic priestess, but was delivered from the occult and the practice of lesbianism by the power of Jesus

Christ. She is now a Spirit-filled believer and is ministering to others in Seattle, Washington.

One of the things Sharon told us recently is that a plan has been formulated by satanists for the destruction of churches through infiltration. Satanists plan to attend evangelical and Pentecostal churches, fake conversion, and hope that their testimony will bring them into the limelight of attention. Once in the "inner circle" of a church, they intend to sow discord and suspicion among the brethren and try to divide the church. We have reports that indicate this may be taking place on a limited scale.

In view of this, we must pray for the operation of the gift of "discerning of spirits" (I Corinthians 12:10). However, we do not want a Dark Ages style witch-hunt manifesting a "gift of suspicion" working in our midst. The answer to the problem is for each of us to stay very close to the Lord at all times.

Dangers of Argumentation

I cannot recall ever seeing anyone saved as a result of arguing. An argumentative attitude works against what we are trying to accomplish. The cultist often has been given a false sense of peace. If you do not truly have the peace of God, what you have looks inferior to him. Why should he trade what he has for what you have if you seem to be distressed? Using sarcasm or making jokes about his faith will not win the cultist.

When dealing with cultists who are trained in argumentation (Jehovah's Witnesses, etc.), you will probably lose the argument, but this does not mean your point of view is wrong. Remember, some cultists specialize in debate.

This does not mean you should not *discuss* matters of faith and differences of belief. It is argumentation and debate that are to be avoided. The average layman is not prepared to argue with a trained cultist whose specialty lies in this area. The Christian layman reads the Bible to feed on the Word. The cultist studies selected texts to "load his guns" to shoot you down.

Prayer With the Cultist

With some cultists the following approach works very well: Say to the cultist: "We both agree there is a God. This God knows everything and hears us right now. He cares about us. Let's pray together for enlightenment." Obviously, this works better with some cultists than others. You must be selective. It works particularly well with Jehovah's Witnesses and Mormons. Of course, you would not use this approach with a satanist! This approach is effective because it shows your faith and concern — and God *does* answer prayer.

Personal Prayer

It is difficult to be a witness if you are not regularly communing with the Lord you are witnessing about. It is the Holy Spirit who does the convicting and converting (I Corinthians 3:6-7; John 16:8-11). Pray *before* attempting to witness. Pray *while* you are witnessing. If you are with another Christian, pray while he witnesses. Pray *after* you leave the cultist.

Prayer in this realm is both intercession and warfare (Ephesians 6:12). Paul says:

"The weapons of our warfare are not carnal, but mighty through God to the pulling down of strongholds; casting down imaginations, and every high thing that exalteth itself against the knowledge of God, and bringing into captivity every thought to the obedience of Christ" (II Corinthians 10:4-5).

A Fitting Conclusion

"But foolish and unlearned questions avoid, knowing that they do gender strifes. And the servant of the Lord must not strive; but be gentle unto all men, apt to teach, patient; in meekness instructing those that oppose themselves; if God peradventure will give them repentance to the acknowledging of the truth; and that they may recover themselves out of the snare of the devil, who are taken captive by him at his will" (II Timothy 2:23-26).

Appendix:
Sources of More Information

The following sources are sound and evangelical, and some, but not all, are Pentecostal or charismatic. You will find materials for study and for witnessing. You may write to each of them for their catalogs. Some have free newsletters that are very helpful.

1. Bob Larson Ministries
   P.O. Box 36480
   Denver, CO 80236
2. Christian Apologetics Project
   P.O. Box 105
   Absecon, NJ 08201
3. Christian Apologetics:
   Research & Information Service (CARIS)
   P.O. Box 2067
   Costa Mesa, CA 92626
4. Christian Apologetics:
   Research and Information
   P.O. Box 1783
   Santa Ana, CA 92702
5. Christian Communications, Inc.
   P.O. Box 80
   Scottsdale, AZ 85252
6. Christian Ministry to Cults
   P.O. Box M-507
   Hoboken, NJ 07030
7. Christian Research Institute
   P.O. Box 500
   San Juan Capistrano, CA 92675
8. Saints Alive
   P.O. Box 113
   Issaquah, WA 98027
9. Professor Edmond C. Gruss
   Department of Apologetics
   Los Angeles Baptist College
   Newhall, CA 91321
10. Help Jesus
    P.O. Box 265
    Whittier, CA 90608

11. Institute of Contemporary Christianity
    P.O. Box A
    Oakland, NJ 07436
12. Jesus People-USA
    4431 North Paulina
    Chicago, IL 60640
13. Jude 3
    P.O. Box 1659
    Milwaukee, WI 53201
14. Modern Microfilm Company (Mormons)
    P.O. Box 1884
    Salt Lake City, UT 84110
15. Religious Analysis Service
    2708 East Lake Street
    Minneapolis, MN 55406
16. Utah Christian Tract Society
    P.O. Box 725
    La Mesa, CA 92041
17. Utah Missions, Inc.
    Box 47
    Marlow, OK 73055
18. David A. Lewis
    304 East Manchester
    Springfield, MO 65807
    (The author has tapes (cassettes) on various
cults and occult movements, as well as Bible
prophecy, and has written several books on various
subjects.)

   This list of sources is by no means exhaustive.
Any good Christian bookstore will stock usable
materials, and will have suggestions on what else is
available. The author would appreciate being
notified of any new information, helpful sources of
material, and personal insights and observations.
Testimonies of deliverance from the occult and cults
would be appreciated. Write to address #19 above.

ABOUT THE AUTHOR

Dr. David A. Lewis received his Biblical education at Central Bible College, Springfield, MO. He has continued a program of auto-didactic education in numerous fields. Dr. D. Lewis is ordained in the Assemblies of God Church.

He received an Honorary DD (unsolicited) from the College and Seminary of St. Paul, Rome, Italy, conferred by the late Archbishop Antonio Dranello of the Old Orthodox Catholic Church.

Dr. D. Lewis is the host of a weekly TV program called PROPHECY DIGEST, the only weekly Christian program entirely produced in Israel, on the PTL satellite network Monday evenings. He frequently appears on the Jim Bakker Program, Campmeeting USA, Seminar Live on PTL S.M., etc.

Dr. D. Lewis is the publisher of two tabloids: THE JERUSALEM COURIER and the PROPHECY INTELLIGENCE DIGEST. The AUDIO PROPHECY DIGEST is a monthly cassette service by Dr. Lewis. He has made 37 trips to the Middle East (Israel, Syria, Turkey, Cyprus, Lebanon, Jordan, Egypt, etc.) He has also travelled in Europe and the Far East.

Dr. D. Lewis is the founder and president of CHRISTIANS UNITED FOR ISRAEL. He is currently president of NATIONAL CHRISTIAN LEADERSHIP CONFERENCE FOR ISRAEL, a coalition of Christian groups. He has met and conferred with senators, presidents, leaders of Israel including prime ministers, members of Knessett (parliament), the mayor of Jerusalem, etc.

Dr. D. Lewis is the author of several books including MAGOG 1982 CANCELED; CAN REAGAN BEAT THE ZERO CURSE?; and co-author of WHERE IS THE LOST ARK OF THE COVENANT?